Result Page Generation for Web Searching:

Emerging Research and Opportunities

Mostafa Alli
Tsinghua University, China

A volume in the Advances in Web
Technologies and Engineering
(AWTE) Book Series

Published in the United States of America by
IGI Global
Engineering Science Reference (an imprint of IGI Global)
701 E. Chocolate Avenue
Hershey PA, USA 17033
Tel: 717-533-8845
Fax: 717-533-8661
E-mail: cust@igi-global.com
Web site: http://www.igi-global.com

Library of Congress Cataloging-in-Publication Data

Names: Alli, Mostafa, 1986- author.
Title: Result page generation for web searching : emerging research and
   opportunities / by Mostafa Alli.
Description: Hershey, PA : Information Science Reference, an imprint of IGI
   Global, 2019. | Includes bibliographical references and index. |
   Summary: "This book explores advantages from text and web mining in
   order to address the issues of recommendation and visualization in web
   searching"-- Provided by publisher.
Identifiers: LCCN 2019031688 (print) | LCCN 2019031689 (ebook) | ISBN
   9781799809616 (hardcover) | ISBN 9781799809623 (paperback) | ISBN
   9781799809630 (ebook)
Subjects: LCSH: Information visualization. | Web search engines. |
   Automatic indexing. | Data mining. | Querying (Computer science)
Classification: LCC TK5105.884 .A44 2019 (print) | LCC TK5105.884 (ebook)
   | DDC 025.04252--dc23
LC record available at https://lccn.loc.gov/2019031688
LC ebook record available at https://lccn.loc.gov/2019031689

This book is published in the IGI Global book series Advances in Web Technologies and Engineering (AWTE) (ISSN: 2328-2762; eISSN: 2328-2754)

British Cataloguing in Publication Data
A Cataloguing in Publication record for this book is available from the British Library.

For electronic access to this publication, please contact: eresources@igi-global.com.

Advances in Web Technologies and Engineering (AWTE) Book Series

ISSN:2328-2762
EISSN:2328-2754

Editor-in-Chief: Ghazi I. Alkhatib, The Hashemite University, Jordan; David C. Rine, George Mason University, USA

MISSION

The **Advances in Web Technologies and Engineering (AWTE) Book Series** aims to provide a platform for research in the area of Information Technology (IT) concepts, tools, methodologies, and ethnography, in the contexts of global communication systems and Web engineered applications. Organizations are continuously overwhelmed by a variety of new information technologies, many are Web based. These new technologies are capitalizing on the widespread use of network and communication technologies for seamless integration of various issues in information and knowledge sharing within and among organizations. This emphasis on integrated approaches is unique to this book series and dictates cross platform and multidisciplinary strategy to research and practice.

The **Advances in Web Technologies and Engineering (AWTE) Book Series** seeks to create a stage where comprehensive publications are distributed for the objective of bettering and expanding the field of web systems, knowledge capture, and communication technologies. The series will provide researchers and practitioners with solutions for improving how technology is utilized for the purpose of a growing awareness of the importance of web applications and engineering.

COVERAGE

- Integrated Heterogeneous and Homogeneous Workflows and Databases within and Across Organizations and with Suppliers and Customers
- IT education and training
- Web Systems Architectures, Including Distributed, Grid Computer, and Communication Systems Processing
- Ontology and semantic Web studies
- Data and knowledge validation and verification
- Competitive/intelligent information systems
- Software agent-based applications
- Data and knowledge capture and quality issues
- Case studies validating Web-based IT solutions
- Data analytics for business and government organizations

IGI Global is currently accepting manuscripts for publication within this series. To submit a proposal for a volume in this series, please contact our Acquisition Editors at Acquisitions@igi-global.com or visit: http://www.igi-global.com/publish/.

Titles in this Series

701 East Chocolate Avenue, Hershey, PA 17033, USA
Tel: 717-533-8845 x100 • Fax: 717-533-8661
E-Mail: cust@igi-global.com • www.igi-global.com

Table of Contents

Preface

BACKGROUND

According to the Internet Live Stats[1], there is more than 55,172 GB internet traffic and up to 66,133 thousands of queries being issued by usage of Google during 1 second.

These stats indicate the importance of Web and searching through its content. For a high user satisfaction, there should be high efforts being made by search engines.

That is where search engines need to provide a list of highly relevant results to a user's query. The list of - usually- 10 results is called *search engine result page (SERP)* and the act of producing such page is called *result page generation*. It is also common to refer to result page generation as an act of recommending a set of results toward a user's query.

HOW DOES A SEARCH ENGINE WORK

In particular, any common search engine would be broken down into three main parts; a crawling section where it gathers available online resources on the entire Web, an indexing unit where the raw data would be indexed to become searchable and finally a ranking unit which is responsible to answer real-time queries from users. We briefly go into the details of each section.

Crawling

Generally speaking, crawling is the action of going throw the content on the Web in order to store any useful (and probably updated) information. This is the fist and the crucial part of a search engine. The collected raw data here would be used in the next two parts for retrieval purposes. Particularly, a search engine would feed a group of primary URLs to its crawler and by finding new URLs, the crawler is able to store and detect new and updated contents.

Indexation

Common search engines index the raw gathered data in order to facilitate users with fast and accurate list of relevant URLs.

The indexed data is usually represented as a *prefix tree* (commonly referred to as a *Trie*) which is an ordered tree with strings as its keys.

Ranking

A search engine would finally perform ranking to order relevant Web pages in a descending order of relevancy to a user upon a search query. In order to successfully rank such results, a common search engine would consider a list of factors for retrieving appropriate stored data from its repository. Factors are included but not limited to: Query category, search context, domain-level link information etc.

Challenge in Web Searching

Diversity in users' queries makes it challenging for search engines to effectively return a set of relevant results. Both users' intentions to search the Web and types of queries are vastly varied; consequently search engines are required to take into account different algorithms to be applied for different conditions.

As a result, there are horizontal and vertical search engines developed to answer users' queries more efficiently. To facilitate users with a set of results, there are Horizontal search engines like Google and Bing which are known as general purpose search engines. The recommendation of the Web results in this case is on the basis of applying different algorithms to the entire collection of Web.

On the other hand, there are vertical search engines which are developed to specifically answer to a user's query in a more focused domain by considering a subset of entire Web. Google scholar and Microsoft academic are two examples of vertical search engines.

Difficulty and Solution in Horizontal Web Searching

Horizontal search engines are known to answer users' common queries, usually referred as *general Web queries*. Although it sounds that all users' general Web queries fall into a single type, there are different searching tasks based on users' queries and intentions such as informational queries, navigational queries, transactional queries, ambiguous queries, entity-attribute queries etc. From all these different types of searching tasks and queries, we demonstrated flaws on the current Web search recommendation and visualization for navigational and ambiguous queries.

A navigational searching is where a user targets a specific Web page by his or her navigational query. This specific Web page is usually referred to as *navigational resource* and the act of assigning a navigational query to its relevant navigational resource is called *navigational resource identification*.

Based on prior researches, there are distinct differences between navigational searching and other types of searching tasks such as its query length, search session duration and search query complexity.

On the other hand, an ambiguous query is the case when a query belongs to more than one topic. The act of clarifying an ambiguous query and correctly return relevant Web pages is called *disambiguation from search results*. There are different attempts for such aim such as word sense disambiguation, diversifying search results and Web search personalization. Withal, none of prior works has taken into account usage of relevant visual factors for the process of disambiguation.

Web Searching and Navigational Query

Distinctiveness of Web searching in general and navigational searching in specific can be shown in followings:

1. *Distinctive Users' Behaviors in Searching Tasks*: Eye-tracking studies (e.g., Marcos, M., et al. 2010, Lorigo, L. et al. 2008, Guan, Z. and Cutrell, E. 2007) show significant differences of users' reactions toward different searching tasks for specific result page generation for each searching task. Nevertheless, retrieving results for navigational searching is not well-addressed according to its definitions and characteristics.

2. *Structural Differences Between Searching Tasks:* This type of motivations belong to the situation where the differences between search tasks make it necessary to reply to users' queries specifically. Entropy-biased model (Deng, H. et al., 2009) indicates that less common but more

specific domains are of greater value to a user. Domain bias (Ieong, S. et al.2012) phenomenon reveals the fact that users' clicks are biased by the domains reputation of a result rather than their relevancy. Position-biased (Joachims, T. et al.) points out the bias toward users' clicks based on the position of the results.

Web Searching and Ambiguous Query

On the other hand, in the case of an ambiguous query, we can outline following facts:

- Around 1 out of each 5 to 6 daily queries are ambiguous (Song, R. et al. 2007, Mihalkova, L. and Mooney, R. 2008).
- Users' queries are mainly short and underspecified (Agrawal, R. et al. 2009).
- Some prior works such as (Teevan, J. et al. 2009) have shown the importance of visual factors for remembering and distinguishing between different Web pages. However, prior works for disambiguation from search results did not take into account the feasibility of using relevant visual factors for a disambiguation task in respect to each result.

Considering above motivations, we can see that ambiguity is a severe challenge in Web searching. Although there are various works to tackle the problem of disambiguation (e.g., Song, R. et al. 2007, Mihalkova, L. and Mooney, R. 2008, Stokoe, C. aa 2003, Sun, J.-T. aa 2003), none of these works have considered using visuality as an option. While the importance of visual cues is proven to be helpful to the users for distinguishing between different pages as well as different elements within a page (e.g, Czerwinski, M. P. aa 1999, Dziadosz, S. and Chandrasekar, R. 2002, Kaasten, S. aaa 2002]), there is a lack of specific visual assistance for each returned Web page in an ambiguous search task.

Difficulty and Solution in Vertical Web Searching

There are search engines developed merely to answer queries in a more focused domain. Unlike horizontal search engines, vertical search engines deal with a more focused subset of Web. These vertical search engines can be developed to answer a user's query toward more specific topics such as music, travel, blogs, forums etc.

Main issues with current approaches to return academic articles upon a user's input are high weight on the citation score and little consideration toward the content of the articles. These issues are supported by the following proven facts:

1. Citation-based systems have low coverage and hence low accuracy (Good, N. aa 1999, He, Q. aa 2010)
2. Citation-based systems would deliberately ignore new and related papers for at least two years (Pohl, S. aa 2007).
3. Such systems suffer from Matthew Effects (Stanovich, K.1986).
4. It also suffers from manual or complex NLP techniques for collecting citation scores (Pohl, S. aa 2007).
5. A full-text recommendation can be aggressive and slow (He, Q. aa 2010).
6. Last but not least, self-citation (Reneta Tagliacozzo, 1977, Hyland, K. 2003) can sabotage the computation of papers relevancy based on their citation where authors of scientific papers cite their previous publications as well as coauthors citing each other works.

RESEARCH QUESTION AND SOLUTION PROPOSITION

Considering aforementioned limitations, following questions arise:

Q_1. How can we build a system which follows the previous findings and applies them properly in order to perfectly make recommendation in a navigational Web searching?

Q_2. Is this feasible to assist users in a disambiguation task by properly visualizing SERP?

Q_3. Is this feasible to use a content-determined approach which does not suffer from common issues in the field, yet benefits users with highly similar1 papers?

In a horizontal Web searching, a typical search engine would look into its index and retrieve all pages that have a user's keywords. Later on, the search engine applies various algorithms to the candidate pages in order to make a ranked list of most relevant to least relevant Web pages.

Similarly, in a vertical Web searching, although the algorithms are applied to a smaller subset of Web pages or to different type of file contents, it follows similar logic for recommending relevant answers upon a user's query as it is done in a horizontal Web searching.

To be able to do as such, commercial search engines use data mining techniques. Data mining has become an emerging and hot topic for a long time. The focus of data mining is to extract and retrieve useful information from a large data set and to reuse this retrieved information in future. Consequently, data mining has been divided into many sub-categories such as text mining and Web mining where the former is the act of extracting useful information from -often- unstructured textual data and the latter is the use of traditional data mining techniques to extract useful information from Web pages and Web services.

Usually Web mining can be divided into three main subcategories, namely, *Web structure mining, Web usage mining* and *Web content mining*. The aim of first subcategory of Web mining is to find the relationship between Web pages via direct links or information, the second subcategory aims to retrieve the interesting usage pattern from Web data in order to better provide the Web-based applications. Last but not least, the third subcategory of Web mining deals with retrieval of relevant information from the content of Web pages.

Lattice-Oriented Recommendation for Web Search Results in a Navigational Searching

Web usage mining refers to the discovery of users' clicks patterns from search log transactions. There is usually a pre-processing phase to clean the data in a search log before using clicks information. Accordingly, by finding a logical pattern within users' clicks, then we can analyze the retrieved patterns. Studies such as (Baeza-Yates, R. aa 2006, Chi, E., H., aa 2001, Kellar, M., aa 2007, Beitzel, S. aa 2007, Morrison, J. aa 2001, Broder, A. 2002) which investigate the users' intentions from their clicking behaviors are examples of Web usage mining in practice.

To establish a mechanism to accurately recommend Web search results upon a navigational query, we conducted a Web usage mining over a well-known Web search transaction in order to define new categories for navigational queries. These categories are then used by our proposed approach to build a URL lattice.

This lattice can be used by *formal concept analysis (FCA)* to retrieve a set of candidate URLs. These candidate URLs are ranked on the basis of their topical relevance. This relevancy is computed based on an algorithm called lattice_lift where URLs patterns and patterns of occurrence(s) of users' navigational queries within those URL-strings are taken into account.

Recommendation and Visualization for Ambiguous Queries

Query-Thumbnail Structural Dependency for Visualizing Web Search Result

The goal of Web structure mining is to discover the hyperlink structure at the inter-document level. Thus, by categorizing the structures of hyperlinks into cohesive groups we can compute the similarities between different Web pages. Two of very common and widely used algorithms for Web structure mining are hyperlink-induced topic search (HITS) (Kleinberg, J. M. 1999) and PageRank (Lawrence, P. aa 1998).

HITS identifies good authorities and hubs for a topic. An authority is a Web page that is linked by many pages and a hub is a Web page that points to many Web pages. These weights are defined recursively. As a result, HITS gives two weights to each Web page, an authority weight and a hub weight. A higher authority weight occurs if the page is pointed to by pages with high hub weights. A higher hub weight occurs if a page points to many pages with high authority weights. Consequently, the initial value for authority and hub weights is $\frac{1}{n}$ for a Web page where n is the number of linked Web pages.

Similarly, PageRank evaluates authority and importance of a Web page based on the quantity and quality of links to that page. Not only for ranking Web pages, but also PageRank can be used for retrieving academic papers. However, prior researches (Pohl, S. et al. 2007, He, Q. et al. 2010) showed that this technique will not necessarily improve the recommendation efficiency.

To find the most appropriate title for a returned result in an ambiguous searching task, we used the structural dependency of HTML tags to a user's ambiguous query Moreover, we used this structural dependency in order to extract a thumbnail as a visual cue and a caption for the corresponding thumbnail from the textual content of each Web page to boost the user experience during an ambiguous searching.

Content-Determined Search Snippet Generation

Web content mining focuses on the "mining, extraction and integration of useful data, information and knowledge from the content of Web pages (Liu, B. 2005)". The content of a Web page is either unstructured or semi-structured text. This is proven that 80% of the Web content is textual. It means that many of the techniques used in text mining such as natural language processing (NLP), machine learning and information retrieval are applicable in Web content mining.

For the purpose of recommending and visualizing Web search results in an ambiguous search task, we decomposed a Web page into different paragraphs/segments and based on the scores of *Bayesian naïve classifier* for each paragraph/segment, we selected the best paragraph/segment as the most appropriate search snippet for an ambiguous query. To do as such, we first needed to first make a logical Web page segmentation and secondly to give each segment a relevance point in respect to a user's query. In order to make a Web page segmentation, the author of this book has used document object model (DOM) tree to traverse the HTML structure of a Web page. Doing so, we are able to form each groups of node leafs as a segment of a page. A figure with a caption or a table is also treated as a paragraph.

In terms of relevancy judgment of each segment, the author of this book took into account the study of Fu, W.-T et al. (2010) which showed that whether a search result is accurate or not, a user is more convenient to choose a result with occurrence(s) of his or her query. Henceforth, considering occurrence of a user's keyword within segments of a Web page can give a good relevancy judgment. Consequently, the author of this book considered to calculate TF-IDF (Term frequency-Inverse document frequency) for numerizing this factor and by applying a conditional probability, hence can get a better measurement for relevance degree of each segment of a page toward a user's search query.

Summary-Based Web Search Recommendation for Vertical Web Searching

Text mining is one of the most common variations of data mining. To reiterate, text mining meant to deal with textual content which is usually unstructured. One of the most common approaches in text mining is to numeric-size the text which is done by counting the occurrences of words in a document and indexing them based on the frequency counts. There are different techniques for text mining which we briefly discuss the most common ones as in the followings:

Information Extraction

Information extraction is one of the most usual techniques of text mining to develop. It refers to the act of extracting useful information from semi or unstructured text. A system that extracts applicants' name, address, phone number etc from resumes is an example of a system which uses information extraction.

Text Categorization

It refers to the assignment of the text documents to the pre-defined categories based on their textual content. These categories are commonly referred to as *controlled vocabulary* where they do not carry any semantic. In some platforms, a document can have multiple categories while in some other, a document is restricted to a single category. Some of the useful applications for text categorization can be seen as: indexation for document retrieval, word sense disambiguation from search results in Web searching, organizing and automatically extracting metadata and maintaining large catalogues of Web resources (Witten, I. H. et al. 2004).

Text Clustering

Text clustering aims to group unlabeled collection of data into cohesive groups. In other words, unlike text categorization, there are no predefined categories and thus, related groups of documents can be linked together. Although text clustering attracted less attention to itself, it has the advantage of dependency from training data that is used for producing pre-defined categories.

Text Summarization

Summarizing a document is the process of producing a condense version of corresponding document. This input can be either an individual document or a group of documents. Consequently, there are two text summarization methods, commonly referred to as *single-document summarization* and *multi-document summarization*. To produce a summary of a document, words within the document should be indexed. Term frequency-Inverse document frequency or in short, *TF-IDF* is one of the most commonly used techniques for indexing words within a document.

To do as such, there are several pre-processing steps such as stop word removal and stemming that might be applied to a collection of texts in order to clean the raw corpus from unimportant but frequently used words and to form word families under a same root word respectively. Each of these steps has several variations and algorithms which can be used according to the context of a system.

From a different angle, text summarization can be divided into two groups, i.e, *extractive summarization* and *abstractive summarization*. Extractive Summarization refers to production of a summary of an input based on the terms frequency with or without weighting factors such as the place of occurrence(s) of a keyword. For an extractive multi-document summarization, an inverse document frequency will be added to filter overly used common words within different documents. Abstractive summarization, on the hand, attempts to produce a human-like summary version of an input. It will not only consider the exact word occurrence(s), but also will consider the synonym and acronym version of corresponding word.

While abstractive summarization creates more accurate and readable summary of a document, but at the same time it is harder to be developed due to the fact that it needs natural language generation which itself is a growing field. As a result, majority of works are done in the field of extractive summarization. All in all, studies such as (Liang, T.-P. et al. 2008, Bogers, T. and van den Bosch, A. 2009) showed that a content-based filtering (CBF) performs better than a collaborative filtering (CF) for recommending scientific papers.

Although using full-text similarity will be time intensive (He, Q. et al. 2010), we can build a summary from the content of each paper and store it as a representation of the whole paper. One might argue that there is an abstract for each paper that is provided by the author(s) of a paper as a summary. Nevertheless, these abstracts are proven to be not a comprehensive summary of the corresponding paper (Elkiss, A. et al. 2008, Bradshaw, S. 2003).

Another critic may argue that a good academic recommender should return relevant papers and citation score is a good metric for such aim. This criticism can be answered by the fact that *the cluster hypothesis* (Rijsbergen, C. J. V. 1979) proves similar items have high likelihood of being relevant too. That way, if a recommender measures the similarity of two papers not based on citation scores but based on the similarity of their summaries, it can eliminate the flaws of a full-text similarity, citation-based systems and other similar academic recommenders while return relevant papers to a user.

RESEARCH CONTRIBUTION

The focus of this book is to take advantages from text and Web mining in order to address the issues of recommendation and visualization in Web searching. Fortunately, this is known that around 80% of the Web content is textual. That means text mining would form an important part of Web mining, specifically Web content mining.

In the context of general Web searching, we picked two directions, i.e, navigational searching and ambiguous queries. We introduced a framework for responding to a user's navigational query which takes into account URLs patterns and pattern of keyword(s) occurrence(s) within the URL-strings of Web pages.

This proposed approach builds a URL lattice which is based on pre-defined categories. Afterward, by applying formal concept analysis (FCA), we are able to build a set of candidate URLs in respect to a user's navigational query. Furthermore, we introduced a weighting algorithm called *lattice_lift* that its aim is to rank the candidate URLs.

Within this work, we conducted two Web usage studies. In first study, we used implicit judgments of users from a well-know query log to define categories for navigational resources. To define categories for non-navigational resources, we used prior findings on domain bias and definition of ambiguous URLs as well as the increase of displays of these URLs by common commercial search engines. Second study is where we conducted a comparative study between two of search logs which are used in this study to elaborate the different treatments toward navigational Web searching by users based on their locality. By locality we refer to the different language preferences that users have while they perform navigational searching.

Additionally, we addressed the issue of visualizing Web search results toward an ambiguous query where the lack of visuality and appropriate search snippet derived us to implement a better framework that benefits users with a better experience in an ambiguous search task.

In the context of academic Web searching, we addressed the issue of paper recommendation by considering the fact that most commercial and in-use algorithms to respond to a user's query are reluctant to the benefits of using a content-determined recommender which does not suffer from extensive full-text relevancy judgment.

Moreover, the flaws of current academic recommenders further motivated us to investigate the feasibility of using summarized version of papers in order to establish an academic recommender that facilitate users with highly similar and relevant scientific papers.

Within this research work, we have implemented two sets of baselines. First type of baseline belongs to a baseline which is based on h-index and estimated h-index score of corresponding author of a paper. Second type of baseline belongs to an implementation of Google scholar based on its dependency to citation scores of papers. We formulated retrieval behavior of Google scholar based on citation counts and similarity of their titles and abstracts with input query.

We further suggested a textual-visual binding for selecting similar papers from common coauthor's publication records. In this way, we guarantee that, unlike current methods, our proposed method would intellectually return similar papers from publication records of common coauthor(s) in respect to the input paper.

BOOK OUTLINE

Chapter 1 is dedicated to a comprehensive literature review regarding navigational Web searching and earlier works on this subject. There are several researches on the benefits on a shorter result page compared to a longer list of results. Since there is only one specific navigational resource to a user's query, results of these studies are more valid in the context of navigational searching. Moreover, eye-tracking studies and other search-log analyses indicated that there should be different treatment towards different type of searching tasks, while state-of-the-art for result page generation for horizontal search engines does not take into account these findings at least for navigational searching.

Chapter 2 belongs to discussion on issues in current navigational searching and navigational resource identification followed by a comparative study between native and non-native English speaking users. To draw accurate conclusions, we performed a comparative Web usage study on two search logs from users with different language preferences. The results of this comparative study indeed revealed differences of treatments toward navigational searching of users with different locality based on various evidences.

In Chapter 3, we addressed the difficulties for Web search recommendation for navigational searching where a user is overwhelmed by load of unnecessary information to his or her navigational query. Consequently we introduced a method to take into account the characteristics of navigational searching for the act of navigational resource identification. To do as such, we considered former studies for Web page clustering based on the patterns of URLs. To introduce useful categories for navigational searching, we conducted a Web usage mining on a well-known search log regarding implicit judgments of users to form similar Web pages into cohered categories.

In Chapter 4, ambiguous queries and disambiguation tasks are discussed. We begun by demonstrating the flaws for Web search visualization for ambiguous queries and we supported our proposed solution by the results of previous works on the effectiveness of visual cues on the remembering previously visited Web pages and distinguishing between different elements of Web pages. Consequently, our proposal for this case includes involving visual cues from content of each result together with generating newly search snippet and title for each result. Results of our two user studies indicated considerable assistance from our proposal for users toward disambiguation from results.

Chapter 5 is dedicated to the introduction of the Bathan, a summary-based framework for recommending scientific papers. We argued the fact that state-of-the-art puts too much of weight in papers' citation counts which brings various issues such as accuracy and coverage. In addition, current content-determined techniques such as a full-text similarity measurement are time-intensive and slow. Thus we proposed a remedy to the current fatigues in recommending scholarly papers which is based on retrieving papers in respect to the similarities of their summaries. Results of our experiments showed higher performance against state-of-the-art according to the evaluation metrics.

We proposed an enhancement to our proposed summary-based recommender by considering textual references to the visual features of one's publication record in order to retrieve the similar papers of common coauthors. We elaborated this proposal in Chapter 6. The critical issues on the use of citation scores as well as the significant difference between an abstract and a summary produced from other part of a paper motivated us to work on preparing a framework which not only cures the drawback of current Web search recommendation on the field of academic Web searching, but also benefits system with a less resource-intensive technique. In addition, state-of-the-art lacks intellectually retrieving relevant papers from one's publication record. Consequently, our proposal targets this absence by considering similarity of text fragments of one's publications that are referring to visual features of papers such as Tables and Figures.

In Chapter 7, we investigated the problem of mobile Web searching. To overcome this issue, we proposed a mechanism to decompose a Web page into different segments in order to find the most relevant part of the post regarding to a user's query. To do as such, we applied TF-IDF to the occurrences of a user query and by applying a conditional probability for a keyword to be occurred within a segment.

REFERENCES

Agrawal, R., Gollapudi, S., Halverson, A., & Ieong, S. (2009). Diversifying search results. *Proceedings of the Second ACM International Conference on Web Search and Data Mining, WSDM '09*, 5–14. 10.1145/1498759.1498766

Alli, M. (2012). *Dom-based automatic webpage scrolling in mobile search system* (Master's thesis). Huazhong University of Science and Technology.

Baeza-Yates, R., Calderón-Benavides, L., & González-Caro, C. (2006). The intention behind web queries. *Proceedings of the 13th International Conference on String Processing and Information Retrieval, SPIRE'06*, 98–109. 10.1007/11880561_9

Beel, J., Gipp, B., Langer, S., & Breitinger, C. (2015). Research-paper recommender systems: A literature survey. *International Journal on Digital Libraries*, 1–34.

Beel, J., Langer, S., Genzmehr, M., Gipp, B., Breitinger, C., & Nürnberger, A. (2013). Research paper recommender system evaluation: A quantitative literature survey. *Proceedings of the International Workshop on Reproducibility and Replication in Recommender Systems Evaluation, RepSys '13*, 15–22.

Beitzel, S. M., Jensen, C., Lewis, D. D., Chowdhury, A., & Frieder, O. (2007). Automatic classification of web queries using very large unlabeled query logs. *ACM Transactions on Information Systems, 25*(2), 9. doi:10.1145/1229179.1229183

Bogers, T., & van den Bosch, A. (2009). *Collaborative and content-based filtering for item recommendation on social bookmarking websites.* Academic Press.

Bradshaw, S. (2003). Reference directed indexing: Redeeming relevance for subject search in citation indexes. Lecture Notes in Computer Science, 2769, 499–510.

Broder, A. (2002). A taxonomy of web search. *SIGIR Forum, 36*(2), 3–10. doi:10.1145/792550.792552

Chi, Pirolli, Chen, & Pitkow.(2001). Using information scent to model user information needs and actions and the web. *Proceedings of the SIGCHI Conference on Human Factors in Computing Systems, CHI '01*, 490–497. 10.1145/365024.365325

Czerwinski, M. P., van Dantzich, M., Robertson, G., & Hoffman, H. (1999). The contribution of thumbnail image, mouse-over text and spatial location memory to web page retrieval in 3d. Proc. Human-Computer Interaction INTERACT '99, 163–170.

Deng, H., King, I., & Lyu, M. R. (2009). Entropy-biased models for query representation on the click graph. *Proceedings of the 32Nd International ACM SIGIR Conference on Research and Development in Information Retrieval, SIGIR '09*, 339–346. 10.1145/1571941.1572001

Dziadosz, S., & Chandrasekar, R. (2002). Do thumbnail previews help users make better relevance decisions about web search results? In *Proceedings of the 25th Annual International ACM SIGIR Conference on Research and Development in Information Retrieval, SIGIR '02*, (pp. 365–366). New York, NY: ACM. 10.1145/564376.564446

Elkiss, A., Shen, S., Fader, A., Erkan, G., States, D., & Radev, D. (2008, January). Blind men and elephants: What do citation summaries tell us about a research article? *Journal of the American Society for Information Science and Technology, 59*(1), 51–62. doi:10.1002/asi.20707

Ferrara, F., Pudota, N., & Tasso, C. (2011). A keyphrase-based paper recommender system. *Communications in Computer and Information Science, 249*, 14–25. doi:10.1007/978-3-642-27302-5_2

Fu, W.-T., Kannampallil, T. G., & Kang, R. (2010). Facilitating exploratory search by modelbased navigational cues. In *Proceedings of the 15th International Conference on Intelligent User Interfaces, IUI '10*, (pp. 199–208). New York, NY: ACM. 10.1145/1719970.1719998

Good, N., Schafer, J. B., Konstan, J. A., Borchers, A., Sarwar, B., Herlocker, J., & Riedl, J. (1999) Combining collaborative filtering with personal agents for better recommendations. *Proceedings of the Sixteenth National Conference on Artificial Intelligence and the Eleventh Innovative Applications of Artificial Intelligence Conference Innovative Applications of Artificial Intelligence, AAAI '99/IAAI '99*, 439–446.

Guan, Z., & Cutrell, E. (2007). An eye tracking study of the effect of target rank on web search. *Proceedings of the SIGCHI Conference on Human Factors in Computing Systems, CHI '07*, 417–420. 10.1145/1240624.1240691

He, Q., Pei, J., & Kifer, D. (2010). Context-aware citation recommendation. *Proceedings of the 19th International Conference on World Wide Web, WWW '10*, 421–430. 10.1145/1772690.1772734

Hyland, K. (2003). Self-citation and self-reference: Credibility and promotion in academic publication. *Journal of the American Society for Information Science, 54*(3), 251–259. doi:10.1002/asi.10204

Ieong, S., Mishra, N., Sadikov, E., & Zhang, L. (2012). Domain bias in web search. *Proceedings of the Fifth ACM International Conference on Web Search and Data Mining, WSDM '12*, 413–422. 10.1145/2124295.2124345

Joachims, T., Granka, L., Pan, B., Hembrooke, H., Radlinski, F., & Gay, G. (2007, April). () Evaluating the accuracy of implicit feedback from clicks and query reformulations in web search. *ACM Transactions on Information Systems, 25*(2), 7. doi:10.1145/1229179.1229181

Kaasten, S., Greenberg, S., & Edwards, C. (2002). How people recognize previously seen web pages from titles,urls and thumbnails. In X. Faulkner, J. Finlay, & F. Detienne (Eds.), *People and computers XVI* (pp. 247–265). Proc. Human Computer Interaction.

Kellar, M., Watters, C., & Shepherd, M. (2007). A field study characterizing web-based informationseeking tasks. *Journal of the American Society for Information Science and Technology, 58*(7), 999–1018. doi:10.1002/asi.20590

Kleinberg, J. M. (1999). Authoritative sources in a hyperlinked environment. *Journal of the Association for Computing Machinery*, *46*(5), 604–632. doi:10.1145/324133.324140

Lawrence, P., Sergey, B., Motwani, R., & Winograd, T. (1998). *The pagerank citation ranking: Bringing order to the web. Technical report.* Stanford University.

Liang, T.-P., Yang, Y.-F., Chen, D.-N., & Ku, Y.-C. (2008). A semantic-expansion approach to personalized knowledge recommendation. *Decision Support Systems*, *45*(3), 401–412. doi:10.1016/j.dss.2007.05.004

Liu, B. (2005). WISE-2005 Tutorial: Web Content Mining. Springer Berlin Heidelberg.

Lorigo, L., Haridasan, M., Brynjarsdóttir, H., Xia, L., Joachims, T., Gay, G., Granka, L., Pellacini, F., & Pan, B. (2008). Eye tracking and online search: Lessons learned and challenges ahead. *Journal of the American Society for Information Science and Technology*, *59*(7), 1041–1052. doi:10.1002/asi.20794

Marcos, M. C., & Gonzalez-Caro, C. C. (2010). de los usuarios en la pagina de resultados de los buscadores. un estudio basado en eye tracking. *El Profesional de la Información*, *19*(4), 348–358. doi:10.3145/epi.2010.jul.03

Mihalkova, L., & Mooney, R. (2008). Search query disambiguation from short sessions. In *Beyond Search*. Computational Intelligence for the Web Workshop at NIPS.

Morrison, J. B., Pirolli, P., & Card, S. K. (2001). A taxonomic analysis of what world wide web activities significantly impact people's decisions and actions. In *CHI '01 Extended Abstracts on Human Factors in Computing Systems, CHI EA '01* (pp. 163–164). ACM. doi:10.1145/634067.634167

Nascimento, C., Laender, A. H., da Silva, A. S., & Gonçalves, M. A. (2011). A source independent framework for research paper recommendation. *Proceedings of the 11th Annual International ACM/IEEE Joint Conference on Digital Libraries, JCDL '11*, 297–306. 10.1145/1998076.1998132

Pohl, S., Radlinski, F., & Joachims, T. (2007). Recommending related papers based on digital library access records. *Proceedings of the 7th ACM/IEEE-CS Joint Conference on Digital Libraries, JCDL '07*, 417–418. 10.1145/1255175.1255260

Rijsbergen, C. J. V. (1979). *Information Retrieval* (2nd ed.). Butterworth-Heinemann.

Sayyadi, H., & Getoor, L. (2009). Futurerank: Ranking scientific articles by predicting their future pagerank. *Proc. of the 9th SIAM International Conference on Data Mining*, 533–544. 10.1137/1.9781611972795.46

Song, R., Luo, Z., Wen, J.-R., Yu, Y., & Hon, H.-W. (2007). Identifying ambiguous queries in web search. In *Proceedings of the 16th International Conference on World Wide Web, WWW '07*, (pp. 1169–1170). New York, NY: ACM. 10.1145/1242572.1242749

Stanovich, K. (1986). Matthew effects in reading: Some consequences of individual differences in the acquisition of literacy. *Reading Research Quarterly*, *22*(4), 1986. doi:10.1598/RRQ.21.4.1

Stokoe, C., Oakes, M. P., & Tait, J. (2003). Word sense disambiguation in information retrieval revisited. In *Proceedings of the 26th Annual International ACM SIGIR Conference on Research and Development in Informaion Retrieval, SIGIR '03*, (pp. 159–166). New York, NY: ACM. 10.1145/860435.860466

Sugiyama, K., & Kan, M. (2010). Scholarly paper recommendation via user's recent research interests. *Proceedings of the 2010 Joint International Conference on Digital Libraries, JCDL 2010*, 29–38. 10.1145/1816123.1816129

Sun, J.-T., Zeng, H.-J., Liu, H., Lu, Y., & Chen, Z. (2005). Cubesvd: A novel approach to personalized web search. In *Proceedings of the 14th International Conference on World Wide Web, WWW '05*, (pp. 382–390). New York, NY: ACM. 10.1145/1060745.1060803

Tagliacozzo, R. (1977). Self citations in scientific literature. *The Journal of Documentation*, *33*(4), 251–265. doi:10.1108/eb026644

Teevan, J., Cutrell, E., Fisher, D., Drucker, S. M., Ramos, G., André, P., & Hu, C. (2009). Visual snippets: Summarizing web pages for search and revisitation. In *Proceedings of the SIGCHI Conference on Human Factors in Computing Systems, CHI '09*, (pp. 2023–2032). New York, NY: ACM. 10.1145/1518701.1519008

Witten, I. H., Don, K. J., Dewsnip, M., & Tablan, V. (2004). Text mining in a digital library. *International Journal on Digital Libraries*, *4*(1), 2004. doi:10.100700799-003-0066-4

ENDNOTE

[1]   https://www.internetlivestats.com/one-second/

Chapter 1
Navigational Searching and User Treatments:
Particularity in Web Searching

ABSTRACT

In this chapter, the authors presented particularity of web searching in the context of navigational searching based on previous studies. Consequently, they divided this chapter into two parts. The first part of this chapter belongs to earlier works that examined eye-tracking studies to investigate distinctiveness between different searching tasks while the second part belongs to the discussion on the structure and nature of each searching task based on the results of earlier web usage studies.

INTRODUCTION

Horizontal search engines are known to answer a user's common query, usually referred to as general Web query. These general queries are distinguished based on their characteristics. To acquire these characteristics, researches are done based on explicit and implicit users' feedback according to well-known search logs such as AltaVista and AOL (American online). In this chapter, we highlighted significant differences of users' treatments toward navigational searching in respect to the other searching tasks.

DOI: 10.4018/978-1-7998-0961-6.ch001

BACKGROUND

In short, a navigational searching is where a user targets a specific Web page by his or her navigational query. This specific Web page is usually referred to as *navigational resource* and the act of assigning a navigational query to its relevant navigational resource is called *navigational resource identification*. Based on prior researches, there are distinct differences between navigational searching and other types of searching tasks which can be grouped into 3 different clusters, namely, *query length, search session duration* and *search query complexity*.

Web community has studied users' intentions in Web searching (e.g., Jasen & Spink (2005), Broder (2002)), based on the principle of Web usage mining or more specifically, Web query mining. Goal of such study is to acquire relevant information from search transactions to improve the quality of information representation. Consequently, results of these studies are used to classify Web searching tasks into 3 main groups, i.e., *informational, navigational* and *transactional* searching. An informational searching is to locate content about a particular topic among one or more Web pages. On the other hand, a navigational searching is where the searcher tries to reach to a specific Web site. This Web site can be that of a person or organization. Lastly, a transactional searching is where searcher may perform some Web-mediated activities to achieve to some product by executing some Web services (Jasen & Spink (2005), Broder (2002)).

NAVIGATIONAL WEB SEARCHING AND USER'S PREFERENCE

Eye-Tracking Study and User's Behavior in Web Searching

Eye-tracking studies can give us a better understanding of how users treat different searching tasks. Google golden triangle (Enquiro 2005) tells us that users read more of higher rank results compared to the lower ones. Study carried out by Marcos, M. C. et al. (2010) revealed that users pay attention to elements of results differently from one searching type to another.

On the other hand, Microsoft studies (Guan, Z., & Cutrell, E. (2007), E. Cutrell, E., & Guan, Z. (2007)) shed light on the significance of navigational searching vs. other searching tasks. According to these studies, search session duration for navigational searching is the shortest.

As a comparison, search session for a navigational searching is one-third of search session duration in informational searching. Another significant characteristic of a navigational searching is for its longer URL fixation. A URL fixation is the time that a user spends to observe the URL of a result in search engine result page (SERP). Taking into account this finding, we can conclude that there is a tight dependency between navigational searching and URL of a Web page. Moreover, if we consider that based on Microsoft eye-tracking study (E. Cutrell, E., & Guan, Z. (2007)) a search snippet has less value in navigational searching compared to an informational searching, we believe It is safe to say that considering the URL information of a Web page plays a crucial part in a navigational resource identification.

Lorigo et.al (2005) conducted an eye-tracking study on the basis of different factors. This study reveals some interesting facts. According to the outcome of this eye-tracking study, a Web searching task is dependent to its type. It shows that an information searching is more than 35% longer in terms of its time span. In addition, this has been shown from results of this study that users which performed navigational searching were more likely to spend more time in SERP.

This is due to the nature of searching tasks. Since users in informational searching are seeking for a piece of information, thus they are not targeting a particular Web page. In other words, an informational query may need to be addressed within different Web pages. However, a navigational searching has a unique answer and consequently, a user seeks for that particular Web page within SERP. That is why URL fixation is longer in navigational searching. It means that a SERP with a better knowledge representation can be of more desire for users that perform a navigational searching.

Web Searching Tasks and Their Distinctions

Based on earlier works, a navigational searching has a shorter query length of 2 terms in average while the minimum length for a query in informational searching is 3. A recent Web log analysis (Eickhoff, C. et al., 2014) reported that average length of queries in the dataset used for this study (a 1 month query log of a popular search engine[1] from Feb 1st to 28th 2013 including over 25 millions of queries) is equal to 2.2, confirming similar measurement of earlier works such as (Jasen & Spink (2005)) where reported 83% of queries of their dataset are with length of 1-3 terms. In the case of search session duration, a user would end search session in a navigational searching as soon as s/he reaches to the particular navigational resource.

We can analyze structure of different searching tasks from a broader angle. According to entropy-biased (Deng, H., et al., 2009) model, users may get more relevant information by clicking on less popular but more specific URLs. Although this model did not differentiate between different searching tasks, we can safely say this case is even more valid for navigational searching since the appropriate answer does not depend on the popularity of a Web page.

There are other research findings which confirm our hypothesis. Domain bias is a principle of users' behaviors where clicks are for the domains with higher reputations (Ieong, S. et al., 2012). This principle indicates that the clicked URLs are not necessarily relevant and thus, domain bias should be prevented. Moreover, other earlier studeis (Joachims, T. et al., (2005), Joachims, T. et al., (2007), Dupret, G. E., & Piwowarski, B. (2008), Joachims, T. (2002), Agrawal, R et al., (2009)) introduced position bias where users click on URLs in respect to their ranks in SERP.

Taking into account aforementioned studies, we can find a tight relation between them. A domain bias is a result of entropy-bias. On the other hand, these findings show that following click-through rate (CTR) cannot be a good predictor for assigning a navigational resource to its corresponding navigational query.

REFERENCES

Agrawal, R., Halverson, A., Kenthapadi, K., Mishra, N., & Tsaparas, P. (2009). Generating labels from clicks. In *Proceedings of the Second ACM International Conference on Web Search and Data Mining* (pp. 172-181). ACM.

Broder, A. (2002). A taxonomy of web search. *SIGIR Forum, 36*(2), 3–10.

Cutrell, E., E., & Guan, Z. (2007). What are you looking for?: An eye-tracking study of information usage in web search. In *Proceedings of the SIGCHI Conference on Human Factors in Computing Systems* (pp. 407-416). ACM. 10.1145/1240624.1240690

Deng, H., King, I., & Lyu, M. R. (2009). Entropy-biased models for query representation on the click graph. In *Proceedings of the 32nd International ACM SIGIR Conference on Research and Development in Information Retrieval* (pp. 339-346). ACM. 10.1145/1571941.1572001

Dupret, G. E., & Piwowarski, B. (2008). A user browsing model to predict search engine click data from past observations. In *Proceedings of the 31st Annual International ACM SIGIR Conference on Research and Development in Information Retrieval* (pp. 331-338). ACM. 10.1145/1390334.1390392

Eickhoff, C., Teevan, J., White, R., & Dumais, S. (2014). Lessons from the journey: a query log analysis of within-session learning. In *Proceedings of the 7th ACM international conference on Web search and data mining* (pp. 223-232). ACM. 10.1145/2556195.2556217

Enquiro eye tracking report i. (2005). Tech. rep., Enquiro.

Guan, Z., & Cutrell, E. (2007). An eye tracking study of the effect of target rank on web search. In *Proceedings of the SIGCHI Conference on Human Factors in Computing Systems* (pp. 417-420) ACM. 10.1145/1240624.1240691

Ieong, S., Mishra, N., Sadikov, E., & Zhang, L. (2012). Domain bias in web search. In *Proceedings of the Fifth ACM International Conference on Web Search and Data Mining* (pp. 413-422). ACM. 10.1145/2124295.2124345

Jansen, B. J., & Spink, A. (2005). An analysis of web searching by european alltheweb.com users. *Information Processing & Management, 41*(2), 361–381. doi:10.1016/S0306-4573(03)00067-0

Joachims, T. (2002). Optimizing search engines using clickthrough data. In *Proceedings of the Eighth ACM SIGKDD International Conference on Knowledge Discovery and Data Mining* (pp. 133-142). ACM. 10.1145/775047.775067

Joachims, T., Granka, L., Pan, B., Hembrooke, H., & Gay, G. (2005). Accurately interpreting clickthrough data as implicit feedback. In *Proceedings of the 28th Annual International ACM SIGIR Conference on Research and Development in Information Retrieval* (pp. 154-161). ACM. 10.1145/1076034.1076063

Joachims, T., Granka, L., Pan, B., Hembrooke, H., Radlinski, F., & Gay, G. (2007). Evaluating the accuracy of implicit feedback from clicks and query reformulations in web search. *ACM Transactions on Information Systems, 25*(2), 7. doi:10.1145/1229179.1229181

Marcos, M. C., & Gonzalez-Caro, C. C. (2010). de los usuarios en la pagina de resultados de los buscadores. un estudio basado en eye tracking. *El Profesional de la Información*, *19*(4), 348–358. doi:10.3145/epi.2010.jul.03

ENDNOTE

[1]   Authors did not disclose the name of search engine or search log.

Chapter 2
A Comparative Web Usage Study of Users in Navigational Web Searching

ABSTRACT

This chapter highlighted the differences of users' behaviors between native English-speaking users and Chinese users as the biggest example of non-native English-speaking users. To do as such, the author of this chapter began by discussing the background of earlier web usage studies followed by a literature review on comparative studies that are on the basis of users with different language preferences. Afterwards, since earlier web log analyses are based on web transactions collected from mainly native users, the author of this chapter investigated the feasibility of generalization of former findings for navigational searching to the rest of the users by comparing two web log transactions from two groups of users with different localities in respect to the state-of-the-art in web searching.

INTRODUCTION

Taking into account the earlier discussion, in this chapter we brought a comparative user study to investigate the feasibility of generalizing findings of prior researches on navigational searching to all types of users. As a recall, prior Web usage studies are based on Web logs which are collected from mainly native English speaking users. As such, we are motivated to see if

DOI: 10.4018/978-1-7998-0961-6.ch002

there could be a possibility of applying prior findings to non-native English speaking users.

Consequently, we conducted a comparative Web usage study based on AOL (American Online[1]) and SogouQ, corresponding search logs of AOL and Sogou[2] search engines. AOL and Sogou are American and Chinese search engines respectively, representing native and non-native English speaking users. Another interesting attribute of these two search engine is the collection time. Both aforementioned search logs are collected by relatively similar time in 2006. Thus, the results of this study can be reliable. Corresponding search logs are discussed in details in section *"Dataset Collection"*.

BACKGROUND

There are prior works which are based on non-native search logs. For instance Spink et al. (2002) conducted a comparative search study between US users and European users. This study revealed that European users perform shorter queries with different topics in mind compared to American users. In addition, some other studies (e.g, Costa, M. and Silva, M., J.2010, Park, S., et al. 2005) are based on logs which the default language of queries are languages other than English.

Aforementioned studies showed significant differences between English native speaking users and other users. Thus, we are motivated to conduct a study which compared two search logs that are collected in similar time spans while the language background of users is different.

To make the outcome of study more useful and reliable, we limited the focus of this study for navigational queries that are issued in English vs. other language (here Chinese).

STUDY DESIGN

To successfully investigate this case, we first needed to make sure that non-native users have a different searching behaviors compared to native ones. Consequently, our Web usage study consisted of two parts; in first part, we prepared an evaluation based on AOL and SogouQ. AOL is a Web service provider based in New York City and Sogou is a Chinese Web search engine based in Beijing. Aforementioned evaluation is discussed in details in section *Evaluation*. Results of this experiment are discussed in *Evaluation Result*.

Second part of this research is a comparative study between native and no-native users. We specifically designed this study to discuss AOL and SogouQ in details in respect to a particular set of metrics. Details of such study are discussed in section *Web usage mining*. Results of this comparative study are discussed in section *Study Outcome*. Finally, in *conclusion* we gave a summary of this study.

Evaluation

Evaluation Metric

To successfully perform this evaluation, we managed to prepare relevant metrics for the purpose of this study. First metric is m*ean reciprocal rank (MRR)* which refers to the rank of first relevant result in a list. Corresponding equation of MRR is as following:

$$MRR = \frac{1}{|Q|} \sum_{i=1}^{|Q|} \frac{1}{rank_i}$$

Where $|Q|$ is the size of query set Q and $rank_i$ is the position of first relevant answer in a returned listing.

Second metric used in this evaluation is *average rank*. It refers to the average rank of URLs which are returned by a particular system and are under the domain of navigational resources. In other words, if a system returns a set of Web pages which are from different URL of a navigational resource, hence it would have a lower value of average rank. The equation for average rank for query q is as follow:

$$avgRank_q = \frac{1}{|P_q|} \sum_{p \in P} R(p)$$

Where $|P_q|$ is the number of pages that a framework has returned within the domain of navigational resource and $R(p)$ is the rank of Page p from the set P.

Evaluation Setting

In this study, we limited scope of navigational queries to the category of *computer*. This way, it will be feasible to crawl a subset of entire Web. To detect navigational queries from other types of queries, we used Finkel, J., R. et al. (2005) that is a library to detect named-entities in English and some few other languages. To filter queries for category of computer, we applied *Jaccard similarity* (Jaccard, P. 1912) and we used DMOZ categories for clustering navigational queries. Currently, the DMOZ data is transferred to Curlie project[3]. Equation for Jaccard similarity is as follow:

$$ J\left(A, B\right) = \frac{|A \cap B|}{|A \cup B|} = \frac{|A \cap B|}{|A| + |B| - |A \cap B|} $$

Where A is a category from DMOZ and B is a keyword.

Dataset Collection

We chose two search logs, namely, *AOL* and *SogouQ*. AOL is a 3 months search log from March to May 2006 from commercial search provider, AOL. On the other hand, SogouQ is a 1 month search log collected by June 2006 from a major Chinese search engine called Sogou. Both search logs are collected at similar time slots so that users' behaviors of both search logs would be affected by similar events. AOL contains 20 millions queries and we could extract more than 2 million fully English queries[4] Similarly, we could extract 2049039 fully English queries from SogouQ. Since SogouQ does not have time stamp, we used a reduced version of it, that is, a one day sample of original search log. This reduced version is called *Sogou.reduced*[5].

Ground Truth

To be able to make any useful analysis, we are required to build a ground truth based on aforementioned search logs. Taking into account earlier studies in Web usage mining, there are various strategies for extracting implicit judgments from users' clicks (Claypool, M. et al. (2001), Fox, S. et al. (2005), Joachims, T. et al. (2005)). Nonetheless, neither of these studies gave a solid suggestion on how to deal with users' clicks in a navigational searching.

On the other hand, earlier Web usage studies indicated some special characteristics of navigational searching which help us to build a policy for extracting implicit judgments from users' clicks (Broder, A (2001), Baeza-Yates, R. et al. (2006), Jansen, B., J. et al. (2008)). According to these studies, a navigational searching session ends as soon as a user finds the appropriate navigational resource. In addition, Agrawal, R. at el. (2009) says that unlike informational searching, there would be unlike further click(s) in a navigational searching after a user reaches to the relevant navigational resource.

Consequently, we took into account last clicks of users as a policy for populating our ground truth for the purpose of this study.

Baseline

We used three APIs of commercial search engines, namely, Google custom search API[6], Bing search API[7] and Yandex XML search API[8] as our baselines for conducting this study.

Procedure

As we mentioned earlier, we filtered navigational queries for the category of computer from both search logs. Afterwards, we used these queries as inputs for each baseline and observed results based on the aforementioned metrics and ground truth.

Evaluation Result

Results of MRR and average rank for each baseline in respect to each search log are illustrated in Table 1.

Table 1. Results of MRR and average rank for all the 3 frameworks for both AOL and SogouQ search transactions

Baseline[1]	N[2]	MRR (AOL)	N	MRR (SogouQ)	N	avgRank (AOL)	N	avgRank (SogouQ)
Bing[3]	124	0.871	24	0.901	278	6.592	76	5.435
Google	125	0.796	17	0.753	291	5.33	62	4.41
Yandex	129	0.75	21	0.777	385	4.3	90	4.093

1 Baselines are ordered alphabetically

2 Number of queries with navigational resources within results of each framework..

3 By the time we performed this evaluation, over 330 of queries out of all 739 queries from Sogou were carried out with Chinese version of Bing.

Results of both MRR and average rank for AOL and Sogou suggests that although the absolute values for MRR (Sogou) and avgRank (Sogou) remains relatively same for each baseline, the drastically lower numbers of exact matches indicates that there might be a different way of users' behaviors between Chinese users of Sogou and native users of AOL.

WEB USAGE MINING

Setting

In this section, we performed a comparative Web usage study between AOL and SogouQ search logs. Consequently, to dig the possibility of different users' behavior of native and non-native users within the context of navigational Web searching, we managed to pick factors that helps for the purpose of this study.

Therefore, we first studied the popularity of navigational queries for both logs. This way, we can find out if different treatments came from different issued queries. Secondly, we investigated popularity of domain extensions. Since there are regional domain extensions, non-native users may click on local navigational resources, i.e., those navigational resources that are hosted by regional domains such as *.cn* and *.au*. This is also possible that the low numbers of exact matches. This way, we can find out whether or not the ground truth extracted from SogouQ resulted into local navigational resources and caused the different numbers of exact matches compared to AOL.

Finally, we compared navigational search session duration between two search transactions. Non-native users may have spent longer time within SERP for English navigational queries as they need to translate the information presented within SERP.

Result

Figure 1 illustrates results of 25 most frequent keywords of both AOL and SogouQ. Taking into account first 3 most frequent keywords, we can see that 2 out of 3 are identical. In addition, 10 out of first 25 most frequent keywords are identical from both search logs. We can see a desire of searching home page of Yahoo from Sogou users while AOL users tended to perform more exact searches on the services provided by Yahoo.

Figure 1. Results of first 25 most frequent keywords for AOL (on the left) and SogouQ (on the right)

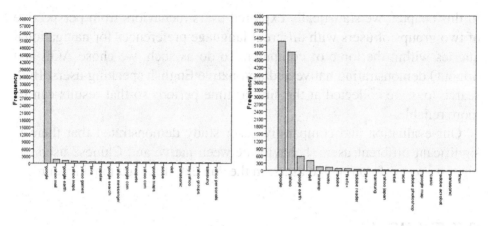

In a nutshell, we can see that both groups of users were interested in similar topics based on their similar frequent issued keywords.

Figure 2. demonstrates frequent domain extensions of clicked navigational resources for AOL and SogouQ. From figures, we can find out that clicks are biased by the users' language preferences on the regional URLs. That is where top frequent domain extensions for AOL search log are *.uk*, *.us* and *.au* representing domain extensions of United Kingdom, United States and Australia respectively. Similarly, top frequent domain extensions for SogouQ are *.cn*, *.hk* and *.tw*, representing domain extensions for China, Hong Kong and Taiwan respectively.

Figure 2. Most frequent domain extensions of clicked navigational resources for AOL (on the left) and SogouQ (on the right)

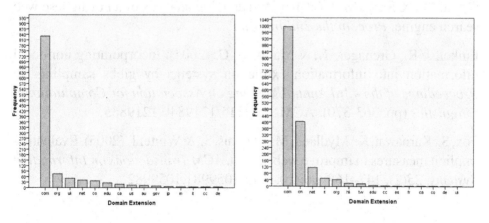

CONCLUSION

In this chapter, we statistically explored users' behaviors from perspective of two groups of users with different language preferences for navigational queries within the topic of computer. To do as such, we chose AOL and SogouQ demonstrating native and non-native English speaking users. Both search logs are collected at the similar time periods so that results can be more reliable.

Our evaluation and comparative user study demonstrated that there is significant different users' behavior between native and Chinese users, as biggest group of non-native users, in the context of navigational resources.

REFERENCES

Agrawal, R., Halverson, A., Kenthapadi, K., Mishra, N., & Tsaparas, P. (2009). Generating labels from clicks. In *Proceedings of the Second ACM International Conference on Web Search and Data Mining* (pp.172-181). ACM.

Baeza-Yates, R., Calderon-Benavides, L., & Gonzalez-Caro, C. (2006). The intention behind web queries. In *Proceedings of the 13th International Conference on String Processing and Information Retrieval* (pp. 98-109). 10.1007/11880561_9

Broder, A. (2002). A taxonomy of web search. *SIGIR Forum, 36*(2), 3–10.

Claypool, M., Le, P., Wased, M., & Brown, D. (2001). Implicit interest indicators. In *Proceedings of the 6th International Conference on Intelligent User Interfaces* (pp. 33-40) ACM.

Costa, M., & Silva, M. J. (2010). A search log analysis of a Portuguese web search engine. *Proc. of the 2nd Inforum.*

Finkel, J. R., Grenager, T., & Manning, C. (2005). Incorporating non-local information into information extraction systems by gibbs sampling. In *Proceedings of the 43rd Annual Meeting on Association for Computational Linguistics* (pp. 363-370). ACM. 10.3115/1219840.1219885

Fox, S., Karnawat, K., Mydland, M., Dumais, S., & White, T. (2005). Evaluating implicit measures to improve web search. *ACM Transactions on Information Systems, 23*(2), 147–168. doi:10.1145/1059981.1059982

Jaccard, P. (1912). The distribution of the flora in the alpine zone. *The New Phytologist, 11*(2), 37–50. doi:10.1111/j.1469-8137.1912.tb05611.x

Jansen, B. J., Booth, D. L., & Spink, A. (2008). Determining the informational, navigational, and transactional intent of web queries. *Information Processing & Management, 44*(3), 1251–1266. doi:10.1016/j.ipm.2007.07.015

Joachims, T., Granka, L. A., Pan, B., Hembrooke, H., & Gay, G. (2005). Accurately interpreting clickthrough data as implicit feedback. In *Proceedings of the 28th Annual International ACM SIGIR Conference on Research and Development in Information Retrieval* (pp. 154-161). Salvador, Brazil: ACM. 10.1145/1076034.1076063

Park, S., Lee, J. H., & Bae, H. J. (2005). End user searching: A Web log analysis of NAVER, a Korean Web search engine. *Library & Information Science Research, 27*(2), 203–221.

Spink, A., Ozmutlu, S., Ozmutlu, H. C., & Jansen, B. J. (2002). U.S. versus European web searching trends. *SIGIR Forum, 36*(2), 32-3.

ENDNOTES

[1]   Based in New York City.
[2]   Based in Beijing.
[3]   .https://curlie.org/. More information on adoption of new environment of Curlie to the DMOZ data can be found at https://www.resource-zone. com/forum/t/dmoz-closure.53420/. The latest RDF files are accessible through https://curlz.org/dmoz_rdf/. In addition, a static version of most recent updates made by Curlie editors are available at https://dmoztools. net/
[4]   Queries which only contain ASCII characters [0-127].
[5]   SogouQ and its reduced version are accessible by: http://www.sogou. com/labs/resource/q.php
[6]   https://developers.google.com/custom-search/
[7]   https://azure.microsoft.com/en-us/services/cognitive-services/search/
[8]   https://xml.yandex.com/

Chapter 3

Horizontal Web Searching and Navigational Resource Identification

ABSTRACT

Generally speaking, horizontal search engines are meant to deal with general web queries. In the context of this chapter, the authors investigated the act of navigational resource identification in the light of horizontal web searching. State-of-the-art navigational resource identification is reluctant to the distinct characteristics of the navigational queries and specific users' treatments toward different searching tasks. Consequently, in this chapter, the authors discussed a new mechanism for navigational resource identification according to previous findings.

INTRODUCTION

In previous chapters, we have shown that there are different searching tasks with significant characteristics. We also have shown that these characteristics may be different for users based on their language preferences for navigational searching.

In this chapter, we introduced a novel approach for answering users navigational searching. In general, navigational searching targets only one particular Web page that is called *navigational resource* and the act of

DOI: 10.4018/978-1-7998-0961-6.ch003

assigning a user's query to its navigational resource is called *navigational resource identification.*

Google patent (Upstill, T. et al. (2012)) is an example of a framework which is specifically developed for such task. Corresponding patent is highly dependent to a query log which brings three issues: firstly, collecting a query log for a query means that a user issued multiple queries to reach to relevant page(s). This fact is stated that query reformulation decreases users' satisfaction (Agrawal, R. et al. (2015)). Secondly, collecting users' data brings privacy issue. Last but not least, using query log makes it impossible to answer newly issued queries.

Taking into account facts and motivations which we discussed here and in chapter 1 and 2, we are motivated to propose a framework which considers prior research findings regarding act of navigational resource identification. Earlier studies have shown that URL of Web pages receive more attention from users in a navigational searching compared to other types of Web searching. Therefore, fundamental characteristic of proposed method takes into account URL information of a Web page for the process of navigational resource identification.

BACKGROUND

In this section, we went through related works in respect to navigational resource identification.

Kang and Kim (2003) proposed to combine URL and content information for the purpose of navigational resource identification. This study assumed that navigational resources are merely home pages which are against prior Web usage studies (B. J. Jansen et al. (2008), B. J. Jansen and A. Spink (2005)).

Westerveld et al. (2001) also tried to distinguish between home pages and other pages by applying some probability models. An interesting finding of this study is that adding URL information to the result of mean reciprocal rank (MRR) improved it from 0.26 to 0.82 which showed the importance of URL information in navigational Web searching. In addition, a part of Google patent (Upstill, T. et al. (2012)) uses URL characteristics incorporate with click-through rate (CTR) data and other evidences in order to successfully apply navigational resource identification. Nevertheless, assumptions made for usage of URL information are simple such as longer URLs are assigned with lower scores compared to shorter one.

NAVIGATIONAL RESOURCE IDENTIFICATION

In this chapter we proposed a framework which uses former findings from Web usage analyses and other evidences in order to more effectively perform navigational resource identification. To make it feasible to crawl a subset of Web collection and to make this study more concise, we only considered navigational queries which are within the topic of computer.

As we stated previously, state-of-the-art is reluctant to use URL information more effectively in the process of navigational resource identification while earlier studies showed that URL information carries crucial information about the corresponding Web page.

Our proposed method has two stages; in first stage we build a URL lattice and apply formal concept analysis (FCA) over the corresponding lattice to make a list of URL candidates. Second stage is where we introduced a weighting algorithm to rank URL candidates based on their <URL, Keyword> dependency.

Formal Concept Analysis

Formal Concept Analysis (FCA) (Wille, R. (1982)) uses a set of *objects (G)* and maps them to a set of *attributed (M)* according to a set of *relations (I)*. A context is defined in the context of FCA as a triple of G and M and I (G;M;I). A concept is also defined as a pair (A;B) with following relations:

$$A \subseteq G, B \subseteq M, A = \acute{B}, B = \acute{A}$$

Where $\acute{A}$ and $\acute{B}$ are sets of all objects that have same attributes and sets of all attributes that are bind to same objects.

To be able to apply FCA for the purpose of this study, we needed to define sets of objects, attributes and relations. Sets of objects can be the collection of URLs that at least have one occurrence of a user's navigational query, M to be set of attributes illustrated in Table. 2 and *I* to be the relations between these two sets. These attributes are defined based on the occurrence of users' queries and length of URL segments.

Researches such as (Blanco, L. et al. (2011), Zhang, C. et al. (2013)) showed that topic-related web pages share common pattern in their URL-strings. Uniformly, a recent research finding (Song, W. et al. (2015)) reveals that Web pages with similar form of URL pattern tend to share similar textual structure. These researches motivated us to investigate this phenomenon to find the possible patterns for navigational and non-navigational resources based on URL-strings of Web pages

Consequently, we used the results of Web usage study in last chapter to

Table 1. Attribute set

Attribute	Remark
D	Complete occurrence of a user's query at Domain level
D'	Only one of the keywords occurred at domain level
P_i	Partial occurrence at the domain level and path level
P_a	Complete occurrence at path level
$P_{a'}$	Partial occurrence at path level
I	No keyword occurrence at the URL-string // occurrence at info tag

define categories for navigational resources. The categories are based on the fact that in most cases, users' clicked on URLs which were conveyed by occurrences of their navigational queries within the URL-strings of Web pages. In next sections we discussed policies for selecting candidate URLs and ranking them in details.

In order to return relevant Web pages, we also defined categories for non-navigational resources based on findings in Ieong, S. et al. (2012) where it showed that displays of pages with high reputation such as Facebook (representing social networks), Wikipedia (representing portals) and YouTube (representing streaming Web services) within SERP has been increased within a year by common commercial search engines. They also showed that this led to less diverse results in the SERP. Considering the case in navigational searching and the concept of ambiguous domains (see section 2.2), we decided to consider these types of pages as a high possibility of being non-navigational resources. Some other similar Web pages such as micro blogs can be also viewed as non-navigational resources since all these Web pages share similar

URL patterns and textual content. Similarity in URL patterns come from the fact that in these types of URL-strings, users' navigational query does not appear at the main domain segment. In terms of content similarity, these Web pages can be seen as an online brochure of the named-entity that it belongs to. Consequently, we described URL patterns for non-navigational resources as shown in followings:

- Portals and Social networks: The URL of this kind is in the form of: foo.bar/.*/user'sKeyword
- Streaming Web sites: The URL of this kind is in the form of: foo.bar/.*/ (aconstant-keyword) + (random-chars-indicating-different-clips)
- Micro blogs: The URL of this kind is in the form of: user'sKeyword. foo.bar/

What these entire non-navigational categories share in common is that the user's query is not at the domain section of a URL-string or there is no occurrence of a user's query at all. In case of a micro blog, the user query is occurred at the sub-domain level and can be recognized easily.

Selection of Candidate URLs

Taking into account the previous researches and the definition of ambiguous URL, we decided to consider least frequent lattice rather the most frequent one. At first step, We need to create a set of candidate URLs to form the URL lattice. To do as such, we make a pool of first 10 URLs from lest frequent concept lattice based on the aforementioned settings.

Ranking Policy

To adopt and apply a weighting algorithm to the candidate set acquired from the URL lattice, we introduced Lattice_laift, an algorithm which considers the pattern of occurrence.

This algorithm takes into account three factors. First factor is the position of the occurrence, second factor is the type of keyword to be matched and third factor is the type of occurrence. For the position of occurrence, we gave higher weight for the keywords that appear at the domain and lower weight for keywords that appear at the path. That is due to the fact that a user's query appears mostly at the path segment of a non-navigational resource. In case of plural navigational queries, we give higher weights to the occurrence of named entities. Empirically, in most cases for plural navigational queries, the first keywords is a named entity which acts like an adjective and the second keyword is a noun, representing a product or service or extra knowledge about that named entity. For example, Google earth, Yahoo mail, Dell computers, Java script, Adobe Photoshop, etc. are example of such cases.

EVALUATION

Baseline and Dataset

Our target for this evaluation is to show superiority of our proposed mechanism over state-of-the-art for navigational searching. Consequently we picked 3 baselines, namely, Google custom search API[1], Bing search API[2] and Yandex XML search API[3]. In the context of this experiment, we considered first 10 results of each framework.

In terms of datasets, we decided to use AOL and SogouQ search transactions with following specifications:

1. AOL search log (Pass, G. (2006)) is a search log collected within 3 months from March 1st to May 1st 2006, conveyed by over 20M queries.
2. Sogou is a Chinese commercial search engine. This search engine has released a search log called SogouQ[4]. It has been collected by as of June 1st to 31st 2006. As we are interested in only fully English queries, we filtered this search log for that matter and has obtained 2049039 fully English queries[5].

Since we need navigational queries within topic of computer, we filtered out raw fully English queries from both search logs and recorded those that are relevant. Consequently, we have earned 549 and 739 navigational queries from AOL and SogouQ respectively.

Evaluation Metrics

Mean Reciprocal Rank (MRR)

To successfully perform this evaluation, we managed to prepare relevant metrics for the purpose of this study. *Mean reciprocal rank (MRR)* is first metric which is used in this study. MRR refers to the rank of first relevant result in a list. Corresponding equation of MRR is as following:

$$MRR = \frac{1}{|Q|} \sum_{i=1}^{|Q|} \frac{1}{rank_i}$$
(1)

Where $|Q|$ is the size of query set Q and $rank_i$ is the position of first relevant answer in a returned listing.

Average Rank

Using this metric, we decided to see in what ratio a particular system returns completely irrelevant results within the domain of ground truth. To do so, we managed to compute average rank of domains that are within the domain of ground truth. A lower value for average rank shows a better ratio of irrelevant results for a particular system.

The average rank of navigational query q can be computed as (Speretta, M. et al (2005), Qiu, F., and Cho, J. (2006):

$$avgRank_q = \frac{1}{|P_q|} \sum_{p \in P} R(p)$$
(2)

Where $|P_q|$ is the number of pages that system has returned within the domain of navigational resource and $R(p)$ is the rank of Page p from the set P.

Cascade Model

Based on cascade model (Craswell, N. et al (2008)) a user either reviews a list of results or click on a result. Consequently, a user is modeled as a binary variable. This would be a great match for our purpose since in a navigational searching a user targets a particular Web page. Thus, we are interested to compute the probability of a user clicking on a navigational resource. This is where we are in need of cascade model.

The general formula for the cascade model is illustrated at Equation 3:

$$C_{di} = r_d \prod_{j=1}^{i-1} \left(1 - r_{d\_at\_j}\right) \tag{3}$$

Where c_{di} stands for the observed click probability -as a first click- for the URL d at rank i, r_d is the probability of clicking a URL at rank i or skipping it with the probability of $(1 - r_d)$.

Value for rd is empirical and as such, we used the results of prior eye-tracking studies in the field of Web searching (Guan, Z. and Cutrell, E. (2007),Cutrell, E. and Gua, Z. (2007)). These studies showed that a URL accounts for about 22% of the time that a user spends to observe a result. In addition, these studies showed that what the probability of each result to be clicked by a user is based on its rank.

These results are demonstrated at Table. 3. As we can see, these studies only tells us the exact value for results at ranks of 1, 2, 4, 5, 7 and 8. For the other 4 positions, we considered the probability value of nearest lower rank. By multiplying these probability values by 0.22, we can obtain the estimated value of *rd* for each rank position. by replacing these values into the aforementioned formula, thus we are able to predict the probability of receiving a user's first click on a URL based on its rank.

Procedure

By using extracted queries from AOL and SogouQ as inputs for baselines and proposed method, we observed the results based on the stated metrics.

Due to the fact that the format of URLs that are returned from each framework is different, we applied URL normalization so that all the URLs that are used in this experiments are in common format. Consequently, we eliminated all the trailing slashes, removed all the *www.* as first domain label, converted all the *https* to *http* and removed the default and index pages with *html*, *htm*, *asp* and *php* as their extensions. Moreover, we assumed that all the URLs included in this experiment are in their canonical form.

RESULTS

Mean Reciprocal Rank

Results of MRR for all the 4 frameworks for both AOL and SogouQ are illustrated at the Table 4. From the results we can see that UGP is slightly better than Yandex and Google and slightly worse than Bing. On other hand, the results for SogouQ indicates that all 4 frameworks returned much fewer

exact matches for queries retrieved from SogouQ compared to those from AOL. Possible reasons could be of that Chinese users needed to translate English SERP or the fact that they do click on the other results even when they reached the relevant navigational resource.

Average Rank

Figure 1. Mean Cd of 4 frameworks. Baselines are ordered alphabetically.

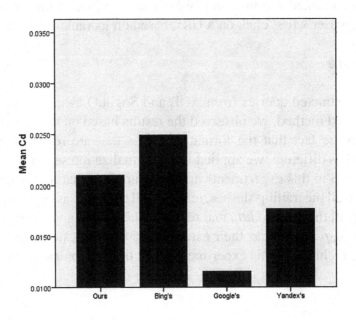

Results of average rank for all 4 frameworks for both AOL and SogouQ search logs are illustrated at Table 5. From the results we can see that UGP outperforms all the 3 baselines with nearly 3 higher ranks position compared to Bing's, 2 higher ranks position compared to Google's and nearly one higher rank position compared to yandex's for URLs within the domain of the navigational resources for AOL search transactions. By the same token, there are still much fewer exact matches for average rank 840 for queries extracted from SogouQ compared with those from AOL.

Cascade Model

Since numbers of exact matches for extracted queries from sogouQ for the 4 frameworks were not high enough for analysis toward cascade model and mutual information, for the rest of this evaluation we only considered to analyze these two metrics only for extracted queries from AOL.

Mean results for the cascade model for AOL queries are shown in Figure.1. As we can see, except for Bing's, UGP outperformed the rest of baselines. In other words, if we only show the URL of results to a user, UGP's list and Bing's would have the highest chance of a user's first click compared to the other two baselines.

CONCLUSION

Selecting and ranking a list of relevant URLs is challenging in the domain of Web searching. Researches on this target are overwhelmed by informational searching and few works are dedicated to the act of navigational resource identification. On the other hand, state-of-the-art for this matter also ignores findings of Web usage studies and distinct differences of searching tasks. Consequently we are motivated to propose a mechanism to select and rank relevant URLs within the topic of navigational searching by considering above mentioned facts.

REFERENCES

Agrawal, R., Golshan, B., & Papalexakis, E. (2015). A study of distinctiveness in web results of two search engines. *Proceedings of the 24th International Conference on World WideWeb, WWW'15 Companion,* 267-273. 10.1145/2740908.2743060

Blanco, L., Dalvi, N., & Machanavajjhala, A. (2011). Highly efficient algorithms for structural clustering of large websites. *Proceedings of the 20th International Conference on World Wide Web, WWW '11*, 437-446. 10.1145/1963405.1963468

Craswell, N., Zoeter, O., Taylor, M., & Ramsey, B. (2008). An experimental comparison of click position-bias models. *Proceedings of the 2008 International Conference on Web Search and Data Mining, WSDM'08*, 87-94. 10.1145/1341531.1341545

Cutrell, E., & Guan, Z. (2007). What are you looking for?: An eye-tracking study of information usage in web search. *Proceedings of the SIGCHI Conference on Human Factors in Computing Systems, CHI '07*, 407-416.

Guan, Z., & Cutrell, E. (2007). An eye tracking study of the effect of target rank on web search. *Proceedings of the SIGCHI Conference on Human Factors in Computing Systems, CHI '07*, 417-420. 10.1145/1240624.1240691

Ieong, S., Mishra, N., Sadikov, E., & Zhang, L. (2012). Domain bias in web search. *Proceedings of the Fifth ACM International Conference on Web Search and Data Mining, WSDM '12*, 413-422. 10.1145/2124295.2124345

Jansen, B., J., Booth, D., L., Spink, A. (2008). Determining the informational, navigational, and transactional intent of web queries. *Inf. Process. Manage., 44*(3), 1251-1266.

Jansen, B. L., & Spink, A. (2005). An analysis of web searching by European alltheweb.com users. *Information Processing & Management, 41*(2), 361–381. doi:10.1016/S0306-4573(03)00067-0

Kang, I. & Kim, G. (2003). Query type classification for web document retrieval. *Proceedings of the 26th Annual International ACM SIGIR Conference on Research and Development in Informaion Retrieval, SIGIR '03*, 64-71. 10.1145/860435.860449

Pass, G., Chowdhury, A., & Torgeson, C. (2005). A picture of search. In *Proceedings of the 1st International Conference on Scalable Information Systems, InfoScale '06*. ACM.

Qiu, F., & Cho, J. (2006). Automatic identification of user interest for personalized search. *Proceedings of the 15th International Conference on World Wide Web, WWW '06*, 727-736. 10.1145/1135777.1135883

Song, W., Zhao, S., Zhang, C., Wu, H., Wang, H., Liu, L., & Wang, H. (2015). Exploiting collective hidden structures in webpage titles for open domain entity extraction. *Proceedings of the 24th International Conference on World Wide Web, WWW '15*, 1014-1024. 10.1145/2736277.2741107

Speretta, M., & Gauch, S. (2005). Personalized search based on user search histories. *The 2005 IEEE/WIC/ACM International Conference on Web Intelligence (WI'05)*, 622-628. 10.1109/WI.2005.114

Upstill, T., Adams, H., I., Lehman, E., Subramaniam, N., Xi, W., & Tirumalareddy, S. (2012). *Navigational resources for queries*. Google US Patent 8,326-826.

Wille, R. (1982). *Restructuring Lattice Theory: An Approach Based on Hierarchies of Concepts*. Springer Netherlands.

Zhang, C., Zhao, S., & Wang, H. (2013). Bootstrapping large-scale named entities using url-text hybrid patterns. *Sixth International Joint Conference on Natural Language Processing, IJCNLP*, 293-301.

ENDNOTES

[1]   https://developers.google.com/custom-search/
[2]   https://azure.microsoft.com/en-us/services/cognitive-services/search/
[3]   https://xml.yandex.com/
[4]   http://www.sogou.com/labs/resource/q.php
[5]   Queries which only contain ASCII characters [0-127].

Chapter 4

Ambiguity and Clarification:
A Visual and Textual Search

ABSTRACT

By the time web engines were developed, the number of queries prompted by users had grown exponentially. This fast growth shows the high demand of users from web search engines. This high demand made search engines responsible for the users' satisfaction during a search session. One way to improve a user's satisfaction is to visualize search engine result page (SERP). Recent studies for meeting this aim focused on a whole page thumbnail for assisting users to remember recently visited web pages. This chapter explores how a specific visual content of a page can allow users to distinguish between a useful and worthless page within results in SERP especially in an ambiguous search task.

INTRODUCTION

Search behavior of users over Web has been extended during time. For instance, when Google was developed by September 1998, it had to deal with ten thousands of searches each day (Battelle, J. (2005)), however, by year 2012 this amount has grown to 1.2 trillion[1]. This dramatic change means that search engines should do their best to improve a user's experience during a search session especially for an ambiguous query. Ambiguity in a search query is the case that a user's search query belongs to more than one search category. Despite the fact that there are vast researches for dealing with this

DOI: 10.4018/978-1-7998-0961-6.ch004

issue, we believe that these methods usually need a user's data engagement tightly to personalize a web search and/or it neglects visual cues for assisting a user in disambiguation task. In addition, there is a possibility that the user intended meaning of the search query may not appear in the Search Engine Result Page (SERP) immediately.

To tackle this, there are numerous approaches. For instance, personalization and keyword extension are two approaches to increase users' satisfaction toward an ambiguous search task. Regardless of effectiveness of such techniques, this can be argued that these techniques still need a user's data engagement which brings privacy issues and neglected visual features for a disambiguation task. To overcome these drawbacks, we introduced a novel technique which gives a user more insight of each result's page content by extracting the most relevant visual content of the page. Moreover, it improves the textual part of the search snippet by engaging naïve Bayesian classifier to retrieve most relevant portion of a Web page regarding a user's ambiguous query.

There are two methods to engage visuality in search snippets to provide users with a better search experience; By 2010 Google has introduced a visual and textual page preview (Aula, A., et al. 2010) to improve a user's chance to make a successful decision to distinguish a previously visited Web apge. This task has been achieved by making a thumbnail of the *whole page* for each URL in search result page underneath each page description/search snippet. This has been concluded from this study that if SERP includes both textual and visual features of a page, it would give the most accurate relevancy prediction for users. However, we believe this can be distractive to face a whole-page thumbnail for every result in SERP.

The concept of Aggregated Search (Paris, C et al. 2010) is another effort to make SERP richer in terms of information representation. The aim of an aggregated search is to collect results from different verticals (such as Image Search Results, News, Videos, etc), while a user searches a query using Web search engines. This way of representation could be confusing and result in a failure if the query has multiple underlying meaning. This is caused by the fact that an aggregated search will not consider the different taxonomies when an ambiguous query is prompted and hence, would return and merge results from different verticals based on the default meaning of the ambiguous keyword. For instance, as we can see in Figure 1, if we search the ambiguous keyword, *Kingfsher* by Bing, the aggregated results only included the default

Figure 1. Most frequent domain extensions of clicked navigational resources for AOL (on the left) and SogouQ (on the right)

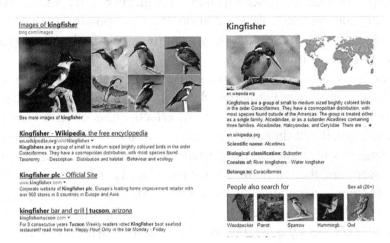

definition of the corresponding search queries while there are other topics related to the searched query.

Prior finding showed that a large fraction of users' queries are short and ambiguous. For instance, Song, R., et al. (2007) concluded that around 16% of all search queries are ambiguous. In a similar vein, Mihalkova, L. and Mooney, R. (2008) showed that 7% to 23% of search queries are ambiguous. That is about 1 out of each 5 to 6 search queries are ambiguous. This illustrated the importance of this type of search query.

Meanwhile, search engines introduced *incremental search* which its aim is to suggest search queries on a real-time basis. Nevertheless, this method seems not being attracted by users. Sanderson, M. (2008) computed average length for search queries and concluded that most ambiguous queries are with the length of one, while there is a considerable amount of ambiguous queries which are longer than 1. On the other hand, Jansen, B., J et al. (2005) demonstrated that about half of search queries have length of 1 or 2.

Other similar studies (Beitzel, S., M., et al. (2005), Fang, Y. et al. (2011)) that search queries are within 1 to 2. Taking into account these results, we can see that first of all, incremental search is not engaged in users' searching effectively and secondly, as ambiguous queries are short and major users' queries are on average length of 1-2, thus, disambiguation from search results is a crucial task.

At this point, we are motivated to introduce a novel presentation for SERP to help to clarify SERP. Our proposed design targeted two problems in current search result page. Firstly, the problem of a presentation that suits for ambiguous queries in specific, and secondly, lack of a proper visual content for pages' description. We addressed these issues by adding a thumbnail and improving the textual search snippet.

Challenges here would be that what picture should be chosen, what is the best position to place the thumbnail and how can we improve the textual content for search snippet.

RELATED WORK

Importance of Visual Cues

Studies such as Czerwinski, M., P. et al. (1999) and Dziadosz, S. et al (2002) discussed the impact of visual features of a page to the users for the task of relevancy measurement. Results showed that visual features of Web pages helped users to distinguish relevant Web pages from others. In addition, it revealed that a combination of text and image helped users to make more accurate decisions.

Similarly, Jhaveri, N. and Raiha, K., J. (2005), Robertson, G. et al. (1998) and Kaasten, S. (2002) claimed that providing thumbnails of Web pages resulted into higher users' engagement with SERP.

Diversifying Search Results

Diversifying is done by producing SERP by results from different taxonomies so that it will be more probable to contain right answer(s).

Yin, D. et.al (2009) introduced diversifying SERP by re-ranking it according to subtopics of a user's ambiguous query. Similarly, Zhang, B. et al. (2005) proposed a re-ranking algorithm for SERP based on link structure of documents and building a graph. Agrawal, R. et al. (2009) proposed to tackle problem of underspecified queries by adoption of a greedy algorithm. Consequently, they expected a user to find at least one relevant result within SERP.

Since there is no graphical assistance for results produced by a diversifying algorithm, thus the possible relevant result within SERP needs high effort of a user to be picked out.

Web Search Personalizing for Disambiguation

By storing search log of a user, Web search personalization tries to predict a user's intention when issuing an ambiguous query. A personalization based on clickthrough data is proposed which takes clickthrough data as input and computes the degree of dependency between users, their clicks and Web pages (Sun., J., T. et al. (2005)). In a similar vein, Mihalkova, L. and Mooney, R. (2008) proposed a short session logging for personalization to prevent privacy issue. Beside the performance of personalizing algorithm for disambiguation, requesting an ambiguous query by a user multiple of times does not necessary contributes to same intention of a user.

Word Sense Disambiguation

Word sense disambiguation (WSD) is the ability of sensing different meaning of a word that has multiple meaning in different contexts. WSD is an NLP problem together with AI and ontology (Mallery, J., C. (1998), Mallery, J., C. (1994)). Stokoe, C., et al. (2003) proposed a sensing framework for disambiguation from IR-based systems. To do as such, they built their framework regarding co-occurrence(s) of terms and applied collection principle to build 3 different variations of their framework, i.e., Term Based (T)-Sense Query, Sense Based (S)-Sense Query and Stem Based which is the Traditional T-F*IDF technique using stemmed queries.

There are various difficulties with a WSD system, i.e., deciding what senses belong to a word is usually a difficult task.

SEARCH ENGINE RESULT PAGE GENERATION

In This section, we first discussed that how state-of-the-art produces search engine result page (SERP) followed by our proposal for visualizing SERP especially for ambiguous queries.

State of the Art for SERP Generation

Commercial search engines usually use *meta data* or DMOZ directories for producing SERP[234]. This may lead to *keyword stuffing* where authors of Web pages try to use popular, and usually irrelevant, keywords to deceive search engines for their relevancy to user's query. In addition, search snippets are usually made of incomplete sentences or textual parts which do not belong to the main content of a Web page. Consequently, we believe that in an ambiguous search task, this type of search snippet and SERP generation will not be helpful. In addition, lack of visual cues for assisting users during search sessions especially for ambiguous queries motivated us to introduce a new way of SERP generation to tackle these issues.

Proposed Method

Since our introduced way for SERP generation consist of adding visuality and promoting textual content of SERP by generating new search snippet, thus in this section we first discussed detecting relevant features of each Web page regarding a user's ambiguous. In addition, we elaborated our proposal for search snippet generation.

Visual Relevancy Detection

Preface

As we discussed previously, visual factors of a page would assist users to distinguish previously seen Web pages. In addition, these visual factors were conducted by users actively. Consequently, we believe that adding relevant visual factors to the SERP will assist a user in a disambiguation task.

Picture Extraction

A picture in a Web page is usually discriminated by <img> tag from other elements inside the page. The main idea of how to extract a relevant photo is the distance of the <img> tag from the occurrence of a user's stemmed search query. The <img> tag is empty; it contains attributes only, and does not have a closing tag. This tag has various attributes. One of the interesting attributes is "alt[5]". This "alt" attribute is used by screen readers[6] to get the content of a page that is displayed on the screen. We took advantage of the content of "alt" for our picture extraction method. Unfortunately, not all <img> are with a useful "alt". As a consequence, we made a priority list for the attributes of a <img> tag, as exhibited in Table 1, in terms of their importance for the derivation of the visual content of a page.

Table 1. Priority list for useful attributes of <img> for photo extraction

Priority	Attribute's Name	Type of Content	Remark
1	"alt"	Text	- It is an alternate text for the image. - Used by screen readers for vocalization.
2	"title"	Text	- It usually shows a "tool tip" when hover the mouse cursor over an image. - Shows an advisory information about an image.
3	"src"	URL address	- Stands for "Source" and speci_es the URL address of an image.

We used the textual content of these attributes, based on their priority, and comparedit with a user's ambiguous search keyword. If a highest priority attribute contained at least one occurrence of the stemmed keyword, we regarded the corresponding photo as a relevant visual cue for the Web page. The zero distance is when the keyword is within the "img", "alt", "title" and "src" textual property in order of importance. If there was no <img> with zero distance from the occurred keyword, we went one node further to inspect the availability of stemmed keywords occurrence until we reach to an occurrence. If there was more than one <img> tag with same distance from the occurred keyword, we applied FIFO[7] policy and appoint the first one that has been traversed.

As we visualized in Figure 2, we offered 4 different templates for positioning the thumbnail together with the page title and search snippet; First is made by keeping the default snippet that search engine provided We placed the driven photo from the page on the marginal of both title and snippet. We call this thumbnail, marginal *thumbnail*. For second template, we improved the textual snippet by the approach that we will discuss in next section. Thirdly, we decided not only to add the thumbnail and improve page description, but also we managed to add a caption for the marginal thumbnails, if it was possible.

Previously, we explained that one way to extract the image from page content is to look at the "alt" and "title" properties of each <img> tag. If the selected picture had any of these, we take it as the thumbnail's caption and placed it below the thumbnail. Lastly, we decided to put the thumbnail as an embedded part for the snippet and put it together with it below the URL.

Figure 2. Four different presentations for the result page. From top to bottom: "Thumbnail with default snippet", "Thumbnail with improved snippet", "Thumbnail with caption" and "Embedded thumbnail"

Belted Kingfisher, Identification, All About Birds ...

Learn how to identify Belted Kingfisher, its life history, cool facts, sounds and calls, and watch videos. With its top-heavy physique, energetic flight, and piercing ...

Belted Kingfisher, Identification, All About Birds ...

With its top-heavy physique, energetic flight, and piercing rattle, the Belted Kingfisher seems to have an air of self-importance as it patrols up and down rivers and shorelines. It nests in burrows along earthen banks and feeds almost entirely on aquatic prey, diving to catch fish and crayfish with its heavy, straight bill. These ragged-crested birds are a powdery blue-gray; males have one blue band across the white breast, while females have a blue and a chestnut band.

Belted Kingfisher Photo

Belted Kingfisher, Identification, All About Birds ...

With its top-heavy physique, energetic flight, and piercing rattle, the Belted Kingfisher seems to have an air of self-importance as it patrols up and down rivers and shorelines. It nests in burrows along earthen banks and feeds almost entirely on aquatic prey, diving to catch fish and crayfish with its heavy, straight bill. These ragged-crested birds are a powdery blue-gray; males have one blue band across the white breast, while females have a blue and a chestnut band.

Belted Kingfisher, Identification, All About Birds ...

 With its top-heavy physique, energetic flight, and piercing rattle, the Belted Kingfisher seems to have an air of self-importance as it patrols up and down rivers and shorelines. It nests in burrows along earthen banks and feeds almost entirely on aquatic prey, diving to catch fish and crayfish with its heavy, straight bill. These ragged-crested birds are a powdery blue-gray; males have one blue band across the white breast, while females have a blue and a chestnut band.

Picture Resolution

In consideration of the original size of an extracted photo from page and the fact that it might be too big for our purpose, we resized and cropped it. We decided to put a photo of 2.1*2.1cm as the thumbnail if in marginal area and for the embedded version, we reduced the size into half. To do this, we first crop the photo by 1:1 ratio and then resized it into a 2.1*2.1cm photo. If the photo had a relatively longer width or height that made it look like a horizontal or vertical rectangle, then we resized the photo to 1.3*2.1cm size or 2.1*1.3cm respectively.

Search Snippet Generation

To make the page description more consistent with a user's search query, we decided to extract most relevant textual portion of the page by adopting *naïve Bayesian classifier*. To be able to do so, we first decomposed a Web page into different segments based on neighboring nodes of a data object model's (DOM) tree. By traversing a corresponding DOM tree of a Web page in a posterior order, we grouped the entire neighboring node at the leaf level, thus we considered them as a segment of that page. Next, we applied naïve Bayesian classifier to all segments of a Web page in respect to a user's ambiguous query to measure their degree of relevancy.

This classifier is based on the Bayesian theorem which is probabilistic and thus it becomes a probabilistic classifier. The simple formula of this classifier can be illustrated as in Equation 1:

$$P(A \mid B) = \frac{P(B \mid A) P(A)}{P(B)} \tag{1}$$

By rewriting this equation to adopt it to our proposal, we obtained Equation 2:

$$P(Seg_i \mid Keyword) = \frac{P(Keyword \mid Seg_i) P(Seg_i)}{P(Keyword)} \tag{2}$$

Where $Seg_i(1 < i < n)$ has a prior probability, $P(Seg_i)$; $P(Seg_i \mid Keyword)$ is Seg_i's posterior probability for given *Keyword* and $P(Keyword \mid Seg_i)$ is the conditional probability of *Keyword* being occurred in Seg_i. In other words, posterior probability of Keyword is equal to a fraction of the likelihood multiplied by prior of Seg_i divided by evidence.

This can be observed that evidence is a constant and $P(Seg_i)$ remains the same for all the Keywords, thus we only need to compute the value for posterior probability of the *Keyword*. Former studies showed that term frequency follows a log-normal distribution (Bruls, M., et al., 1999; Baayen, H.,1991), thus the value of $P(Seg_i \mid Keyword)$ can be computed by applying naïve Bayesian classifier based on a Normal distribution as in Equation 3:

$$P(Seg_i \mid Keyword) = \frac{1}{\sqrt{2\pi\sigma_i^2}} e^{\frac{-\left(tf(Seg_i, KEyword)*idf(Seg_i, Keyword) - \mu_i\right)^2}{2\sigma_i^2}} \tag{3}$$

In information retrieval, a word's *tf-idf* (term frequency- inverse document frequency) is often used as a weighting factor, statistically reflecting how important the word is to a document in a collection or corpus. The tf-idf value increases proportionally to the number of times the word appears in the document, but is offset by the frequency of the word in the corpus, which helps to control for the fact that some words are generally more common than others.

Here, we applied the stemmed tf*idf principle, and for each Seg_i and its stemmed root Keword, we computed the tf value, $tf(Seg_i| Keyword)$ as number of occurrence(s) of *keyword* within Seg_i and idf(Segi;Keyword) as the inverse of the total number of Keyword appearing in all parts. In this way, we can obtain the $mean_i$ and $variance_i$ of keywords' tf*idf values in Seg_i by averaging all the tf*idf values of Keywords in $part_i$ and their deviation from the mean value.

In Equation 2, as the denominator P(Keyword) is independent of Seg_i, and $P(Seg_i)$ remains the same for all keywords, the likelihood that a search Keyword appears in Seg_i, $P(Keyword| Seg_i)$. dominates the posterior probability $P(Seg_i| Keyword)$. As a demonstration, we illustrate the same result page, shown in Figure 1 in our most welcomed method by participant of our user study, the Thumbnail with caption presentation in Figure 3:

USER STUDY

The aim of this user study is to make a comparison between our proposal for SERP generation against state-of-the-art. We conducted this user study by engaging 39 participants. The youngest participant was 18 and the oldest was 50. There were 23 Males and 16 Females involved in this user study. Most of participants were students as well as teachers. However the majority of participants had no background academic knowledge of computer science. As a result, the user study's results will show more realistic results from point of view of common users.

Participants were asked to review our 4 different models and compare them together and with the default demonstration. To do that, we applied our algorithm for two ambiguous queries prompted in two common search engines, one for Yahoo! and one for Bing. For some reasons, like the ease of comparison, we left the title unchanged. Each participant after reviewing all the methods and making a comparison between them, were asked to answer the following questions:

1. Based on the changes we introduced, was there any assist for you to find a most desirable result?
2. Which representation, including the current technique, was best fitted for information representation? If you find our methods useful, which of the 4 suggested techniques looks more desirable?
3. Do you think that the improvement on snippet was helpful?

RESULT

A summarization of the results is shown in the Figure 3. 53.8% of all participants selected the marginal thumbnail with caption as their favorable choice. Their idea was that this method is similar to the embedded one, but it works better when the smaller photo in embedded mode is not as clear as the marginal one. As a result, the larger marginal thumbnail together with the caption helped them more to

find about the content of the Web page. One of the participants said that not only the improvement for textual snippet was great, but also the default snippet with bolded keywords and the title are not really helpful. Notwithstanding, it has been mentioned that although this style of representation is more agreeable compare to others, but the long caption makes the result page with too much of information and hence, not so concise and may e_ect the user negatively. From this comment, we can solve this minor issue by adjusting a threshold to the length of the caption.

On the other side, 33.3% privileged the embedded method and the main reason was its compact structure which includes thumbnail and the improved snippet as well as using the space more efficiently. Also there was an opinion that the one with caption fits a large screen device's better while the embedded lay out is good for handled devices. And finally, 92.3% of all parties found the improvement of the textual snippet useful, while only 7.7% preferred to be with classical page description. From the user study results and parties opinion we can make this closure that both visual and textual aspects are vital to the users for disambiguation the search result page if the visual feature of the page content surrounds with pertinent textual description.

Figure 3. Summary of the results of the user study

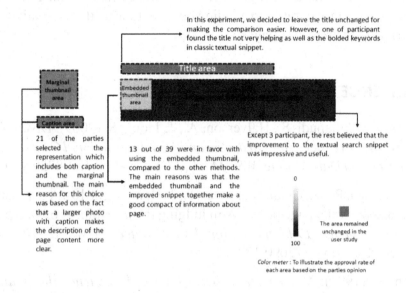

In this experiment, we decided to leave the title unchanged for making the comparison easier. However, one of participant found the title not very helping as well as the bolded keywords in classic textual snippet.

Marginal thumbnail area

Title area

Embedded thumbnail area

Caption area

21 of the parties selected the representation which includes both caption and the marginal thumbnail. The main reason for this choice was based on the fact that a larger photo with caption makes the description of the page content more clear.

13 out of 39 were in favor with using the embedded thumbnail, compared to the other methods. The main reasons was that the embedded thumbnail and the improved snippet together make a good compact of information about page.

Except 3 participant, the rest believed that the improvement to the textual search snippet was impressive and useful.

0

100

The area remained unchanged in the user study

Color meter : To illustrate the approval rate of each area based on the parties opinion

CONCLUSION

Web searching has grown during years exponentially. This is due to the advanced search engines with relevant result upon a search query. However, there might be a chance of misinterpretation when the keyword(s) of any particular query has multiple meaning. In this case, the search engine is supposed to deal with this situation to give the user the best satisfaction. Regarding to this fact, there are numerous researches that has been done to deal with this situation such as, Diversifying the search results, Word sense disambiguation and personalized web searching. Regardless of the effectiveness of these techniques, there is still a gap between the conceptual-textual improvement and visual representation of SERP. We believe that visuality for returned URLs is being forgotten while it has an important role for users to distinguish between relevant and irrelevant results. Besides, we still think that the textual part of a returned page is not informative and helpful enough. These facts motivated us to seek for a better solution to make a better SERP demonstration. At this point, we came up with a novel solution to enhance the information richness of result page demonstration by both adding a relevant extracted photo of the page as a thumbnail to the returned page for each URL as well as improving the textual snippet itself. Our user study shows that visual element for disambiguation is settled and plays a critical role. In addition, to boost the effect of visuality of the page result, improving the textual snippet seems undoubted. Adding to this, a thumbnail with an accurate surrounding text will tune up the user satisfaction for clarifying the returned pages.

REFERENCES

Agrawal, R., Gollapudi, S., Halverson, A., & Ieong, S. (2009). Diversifying search results. In *Proceedings of the Second ACM International Conference on Web Search and Data Mining, WSDM '09*. ACM. 10.1145/1498759.1498766

Aula, A., Khan, R. M., Guan, A., Fontes, P., & Hong, P. (2010). A comparison of visual and textual page previews in judging the helpfulness of web pages. *Proceedings of the 19th International Conference on World Wide Web, WWW'10*. 10.1145/1772690.1772697

Baayen, H. (1991). *A stochastic process for word frequency distributions*. Academic Press.

Battelle, J. (2005). *The Search: How Google and Its Rivals Rewrote the Rules of Business and Transformed Our Culture*. New York: Portfolio.

Beitzel, S. M., Jensen, E. C., Chowdhury, A., Grossman, D., & Frieder, O. (2004). Hourly analysis of a very large topically categorized web query log. *Proceedings of the 27th Annual International ACM*. 10.1145/1008992.1009048

Bota, H., Zhou, K., Jose, J. M., & Lalmas, M. (2014). *Composite retrieval of heterogeneous web search*. doi:10.1145/2566486.2567985

Bruls, M., Huizing, K., & van Wijk, J. (1999). Squarified treemaps. *Proceedings of the Joint Eurographics and IEEE TCVG Symposium on Visualization*, 33–42.

Czerwinski, M. P., van Dantzich, M., Robertson, G., & Homan, H. (1999). The contribution of thumbnail image, mouse-over text and spatial location memory to web page retrieval in 3D. Proc. Human-Computer Interaction INTERACT '99, 163-170.

Dziadosz, S., & Chandrasekar, R. (2002). Do thumbnail previews help users make better relevance decisionsabout web search results? In *Proceedings of the 25th Annual International ACM SIGIR Conference on Research and Development in Information Retrieval, SIGIR '02*. ACM. 10.1145/564376.564446

Fang, Y., Somasundaram, N., Si, L., Ko, J., & Mathur, A. P. (2011). Analysis of an expert search query log. In *Proceedings of the 34th International ACM SIGIR Conference on Research and Development in Information Retrieval, SIGIR '11*. ACM. 10.1145/2009916.2010113

Jansen, B., J., Spink, A., Pedersen., J. (2005). A temporal comparison of altavista web searching: Research articles. *J. Am. Soc. Inf. Sci. Technol., 56*(6), 559-570.

Jhaveri, N., & Raiha, K. J. (2005). The advantages of crosssession web workspace. *Proc. CHI 2005*.

Kaasten, S., Greenberg, S., & Edwards, C. (2002). How people recognize previously seen web pages from titles,urls and thumbnails. In X. Faulkner, J. Finlay, & F. Detienne (Eds.), People and computers XVI (Proc. Human Computer Interaction), (pp. 247-265). Academic Press.

Mallery, J. C. (1998). *Thinking about foreign policy: Finding an appropriate role for artificial intelligence computer* (Master's thesis). MIT Political Science Department.

Mihalkova, L., & Mooney, R. (2008). Search query disambiguation from short sessions. *Beyond Search: Computational Intelligence for the Web Workshop at NIPS*.

Paris, C., Wan, S., & Thomas, P. (2010). Focused and aggregated search: A perspective from natural language generation. *Information Retrieval, 13*(5), 434–459.

Robertson, G., Czerwinski, M., Larson, K., Robbins, D. C., Thiel, D., & van Dantzich, M. (1998). Data mountain: Using spatial memory for document management. In *Proceedings of the 11th Annual ACM Symposium on User Interface Software and Technology, UIST '98*. ACM. 10.1145/288392.288596

Sanderson, M. (2008). Ambiguous queries: Test collections need more sense. In *Proceedings of the 31st Annual International ACM SIGIR Conference on Research and Development in Information Retrieval, SIGIR '08*. ACM. 10.1145/1390334.1390420

Song, R., Luo, A., Wen, J. R., Yu, Y., & Hon, H. W. (2007). Identifying ambiguous queries in web search. In *Proceedings of the 16th International Conference on World Wide Web, WWW '07*. ACM. 10.1145/1242572.1242749

Stokoe, C., Oakes, M. P., & Tait, J. (2003). Word sense disambiguation in information retrieval revisited. In *Proceedings of the 26th Annual International ACM SIGIR Conference on Research and Development in Informaion Retrieval, SIGIR '03*. ACM. 10.1145/860435.860466

Sun, J. T., Zeng, H. J., Liu, H., Lu, Y., & Chen, Z. (2005). Cubesvd: A novel approach to personalized web search. In *Proceedings of the 14th International Conference on World Wide Web, WWW '05*. ACM. 10.1145/1060745.1060803

Yin, D., Xue, Z., Qi, X., & Davison, B. D. (2009). Diversifying search results with popular subtopics. *Proceedings of the Eighteenth Text Retrieval Conference (TREC 2009)*.

Zhang, B., Li, H., Liu, Y., Ji, L., Xi, W., Fan, W., Chen, Z., & Ma, W. Y. (2005). Improving web search results using a_nity graph. In *Proceedings of the 28th Annual International ACM SIGIR Conference on Research and Development in Information Retrieval, SIGIR '05*. ACM. 10.1145/1076034.1076120

ENDNOTES

[1]   Google zeitgest 2012.
[2]   Review your page titles and snippets, By Google.
[3]   Live Search (MSN Search) Guidelines.
[4]   Content quality guidelines, By Yahoo!
[5]   Stands for alternative and is used as an alternative text for an image in a web page.
[6]   Screen readers are usually used by blind people to identify the content of whatever is displayed on the screen.
[7]   First In First Out.

Chapter 5

Vertical Result Page Generation for Academic Web Searching:
A Summary–Based Approach

ABSTRACT

Vertical search engines are meant for answering a user's web query within a specific domain such as news, media, and academic web searching. One main difference between vertical and horizontal web searching is that in vertical web searching, unlike horizontal web searching, a subset of entire web is engaged. The chapter investigates the state-of-the-art in academic web searching and points out shortcomings in this particular domain. Lastly, the authors aimed to propose a summary-based recommender to respond to a user's query by retrieving and ranking them according to their similarity merits on the basis of papers' summaries. Results of the evaluations revealed the fact that the proposed framework has outperformed the state-of-the-art in different metrics such as unanimous ranks and F1 measures.

INTRODUCTION

A comprehensive study is always a hard target to achieve considering the huge amount of online documents available. As a result, numerous approaches have been introduced to overcome this difficulty by recommender systems

DOI: 10.4018/978-1-7998-0961-6.ch005

based on user profile (Hong, K. et al. 2013a, Hong, K. et al. 2013b), using citation data to recommend scholarly documents (Ma. N et al. 2008, Bogers, T. and van den Bosch, A. 2008), a combination of page rank algorithm and citation network (Nykl, M. et al. 2014). In the meantime, we can argue the correctness of these systems based on previous findings (Vellino, A. 2010, He, Q et al. 2010) that using page rank values will not necessarily improve relevancy judgments as well as user profiling in the context of scholarly recommendation would lead to prepare a huge set of data to work with.

In the meantime, a citation-based recommender, i.e., a recommender which considers quality of a paper by counting its citation score, suffers from several issues based on the following facts:

- Pohl, S. et al (2007) showed that a paper needs at least 2 years for gaining enough citation scores for being considered by a citation-based scholarly recommender. This means that a new and relevant paper will be ignored for at least 2 years.
- In addition, *Matthew Effects* (Stanovich, K., E. 1986, Merton, R., K. 1986) would be another critical issue of such systems were a paper with more citation counts would always get more attention and more cites while a relevant paper with less citation score will be otherwise.
- Accuracy will be another spot for a citation-based recommender. This is shown that coverage of a recommender is a critical factor for its accuracy (Good, N. et al. 1999). This is also proven that a citation-based recommender ignores a huge set of documents (He, Q. et al. 2010). As a result, the coverage would be degraded as well.
- These systems also suffer from manual or complicated NLP techniques (Pohl, S. et al 2007).
- Finally, *self-citation* may affect the recommendation process in a negative way where authors and/or coauthor(s) of scientific papers cite each others' publications (Hyland, K. 2003, Tagliacozzo, R. 1977)

Consequently, we are motivated to introduce a recommender which does not suffer from stated issues. We proposed to use summary of a paper as a metric for relevancy judgment. This has been proven that a full-text metric for the aim of scholarly recommendation is slow and time-intensive (He, Q et al. 2010). As a result, using summary of a paper will be a good substitute.

Since our recommender uses textual content of papers, consequently issues of state-of-the-art are avoided.

To make a descent recommender to recommend papers based on summarization merits, we need to establish a suitable summarization policy.

Meanwhile, The cluster hypothesis (Rijsbergen, C. J. V. 1979) similar items are highly likely to be relevant too. As a result, finding similar documents based on their textual content will lead to relevant documents as well.

LITERATURE REVIEW

Scientific Paper Recommendation

Scholarly Recommendation by Using Citation Data

Google scholar as a common academic search engine recommends a list of documents upon a user's query. Google scholar is one of the first and most famous systems which puts high weight on the citation scores in the field of scholarly recommendation [62, 63].

Taking into account information on Google scholar official Web site3, there is a paragraph discussing how Google scholar retrieves and ranks documents:

Google Scholar aims to rank documents the way researchers do, weighing the full text of each document, where it was published, who it was written by, as well as how often and how recently it has been cited in other scholarly literature.

Gipp et al. (2015) has made effort to improve the classical keyword-based searching by introducing a hybrid recommending system which uses more factors for document preference such as citation analysis, author analysis, source analysis, implicit ratings and explicit ratings. Therefore, the recommender accepts six inputs, i.e, text, references, authors, sources, ratings and documents which at least one of them must be provided by the user. Accordingly, using these inputs, the proposed system will provide users with a list of relevant papers. The main drawback of this system is the user engagement for recommendation.

A Co-training approach is suggested for topic classification based on the citation and text of a research paper. The main task of proposed approach is to classify papers that are bound in a citation network. To evaluate the performance of corresponding system, authors of the paper categorized their data set into 5 groups, i.e., AI, IR, DB, ML and HCI. Accordingly, using text and citation information of each paper they evaluated their system.

Although this work does not explicitly targets the paper recommendation, but classified papers can enhance the recommendation. Having this in mind, the evaluation over their data set showed that AI topic is the hardest to be classified for being too general and having few instances1 in the data set. These two cons greatly affect the usage of such system.

Personalized Recommendation Systems for Research Papers

This method can be divided into 3 sub-categories: A tag-based approach is introduced to recommend papers based on the pre-defined tags provided by users. These tags are used by the system to allocate different categories for different papers. Moreover, a self-tagged paper provided by user can be used as an input. Therefore, the recommender uses these tags as a profile for each users, which will be used for paper recommendation afterward.

Personalization can be also implemented by a key-phrased system. Such method assumes that a user is dealing with a quantity of documents which are tagged. Using these tags, the system provides a user profile to match the user interests with the available documents.

Using a concept tree is another way to seek for a user's interests that is discussed in. This is done by applying an activation model to look for users' interests in an ontology graph.

Stated systems suffer from additional data which is highly important to the process of paper recommendation. In addition, this required data is usually provided by users. Moreover, this is shown that building a user profile needs a huge set of data and

Source Independent Framework

Authors of (Veillino, 2009) developed a system which uses a single paper to make the recommendation independent from resources that are needed by common recommenders. This system uses several techniques to generate a list of candidate queries such as n-grams and part of speech tagging (POST). Thus a candidate set of papers is generated and ranked by sending these candidate queries to other existing systems. For generating candidate queries, proposed recommender analyzes an input paper and counts the frequency of terms which are weighted based on their positions. While this method looks interesting, however the focus of work is heavily on query generation and left the retrieving and ranking of extracted documents mainly to other existing systems and search engines.

Using Collaborative and Content-based Filtering in a Digital Library

Vellino (2009) suggested a collaborative system to recommend research papers for producing numerical rating rather boolean rating that TechLens+[67] produces. Therefore, they use Page Rank values in their algorithm. The expectation of the result was to enhance the recommendation results for research papers. However, the author of the paper mentioned that the evaluation results shown that Page Rank values notably decreased the quality of recommendation.

Vellino (2009) is suggested as a research paper recommender which uses a content-based filtering (CBF) approach over its digital library. This recommender requires users to build a mind map for the system in order to enrich the information repository of the recommender 1 and using this mind map together by applying various CBF techniques, therefore the system retrieves a list of related papers.

CiteULike is a search engine that applies two collaborative filtering (CF) algorithms, called user-based filtering and item-based filtering where in former, the system tries to match the active user with neighboring users and in latter, filtering is done by finding neighboring similar items.

A paper recommendation is introduced in where a user-item matrix is in charge of matching users with corresponding papers in a collaborative filtering theme. The idea is that users whom are interested in same area, tend to read similar articles. However, the cold-start is a typical disadvantage. Moreover, recommending based one users' interests1 will result into a huge set of irrelevant papers if users are working on a wide range of topics.

In general, a CF recommender hardly reaches to the expected performance when the number of users is small. Moreover, it has been shown that a CBF recommender performs better than a CF recommender.

NLP-based Paper Recommendation

An Elsevier paper matching is proposed for specifically recommend papers from Elsevier database. The introduced search engine uses a variety of Natural Language Processing (NLP) techniques to build an annotation for each paper. Regardless of the proposed approach throughput, there are two main cons that dominate the whole system's usefulness: It is established to work solely for Elsevier journal papers while there are tons of other outlets that are missing and secondly, the system accepts only the abstract of a paper as an input text. These cons are besides the fact that their ranking algorithm needs at least 100 sample papers for each Elsevier journal in order to be able to give any results. That is the proposed recommender cannot even work well with its fixed theme.

A research data set matcher is introduced to use content and author based similarity as metrics for finding user's interests in order to retrieve relevant papers. As for content based similarity, the recommender uses simple NLP techniques to rank documents based on user's interests2 . In next step, the author names of retrieved papers will be used to add new papers to the candidate set and accordingly, the whole candidate set will be re-ranked based on the normalized Google distance (NGD) value. However, relying merely on Google scholar snippets may lead to miss valuable information and misjudging the system performance. In addition, few publications of junior researchers will be a pitfall of the system since this makes it difficult to accurately judge the current user's interests.

Recommendation Based on the User's Interest

Sugiyama et al. (2011) introduced a key-phrase based system to recommend papers based on the users' interests by considering his/her other publication records. To do such, the proposed system builds up a user profile of researchers based on their publication record as either senior1 or junior2 researchers.

As this is mentioned, this system requires additional data for producing users' profile. Moreover, such system has even a much bigger problem. If we rely solely on someone's publication, there is no necessity for someone to narrow down his/her researching field to one or few topics. It is common that someone changes its working direction after an accomplishment or achievement. Authors has mentioned that they would put more weight (near to 1) for recent papers and less weight(near to 0) for older papers to fix this issue. Nonetheless, this is still possible that an author is already finished its work with some recent publication and has started a new topic.

Recommendation Based on the Correlation of Papers' Similar Factors

He et al. (2010) proposed a context-aware system to recommend citation for a citation placeholder. The method will retrieve a large body of papers based on some aspects such as papers with most title and abstract similarity, papers that have similar authors with original paper etc. The time is one of the most drawbacks of this proposed system due to the fact that the corresponding recommender needs 50-100 seconds time for every new candidate paper. Moreover, they do not consider any constraint for adding authors' papers to the candidate set. Consequently, there will be a large number of unnecessary papers that are added to the candidate set.

Prediction of Authors' Similarity

Applying Coauthor Network

Using coauthor network for predicting similarity of authors can be divided into 3 techniques:

A coauthor similarity system is where the system tries to find similarities between users' and authors' interests according to their research concerns. Such system may or may not recommend papers based on this similarity, however, in case of recommendation, the system will retrieve many irrelevant papers specially when predicted authors are working on a wide range of topics.

He et al. (2010) introduced a recommender system which uses coauthoring network to suggest authors with similar interests. Upon receiving a query from user, the recommender will build a coauthoring networking from CiteSeerX database. Nevertheless, this system will not suggest any similar paper to the users.

A bib network is suggested to predict similarity of two authors using PathPredict. This method seeks for different types of relations that two authors may share, e.g, publishing in same venue, publishing same paper, citing each others paper etc. Afterwards, by applying a logistic regression model, their system hopes to predict the similarity of two given authors.

Building Researcher Network

Teufel, S. and Moens, M 2002 proposed to mine social network of researchers. The aim of this work is to collect researches data from web and by mining the semantic part of the retrieved data, the corresponding framework will build a profile for each researcher which contains common information of authors such as their publications, affiliations, emails etc. In addition, this system, which is called ArnetMiner, provides name disambiguation when there are several researchers with same name or same abbreviated name. For name disambiguation task, ArnetMiner applies a constraint policy which maps 6 constraints, i.e, CoOrganization, CoAuthor, Citation, CoEmail,FeedBack from users and t-CoAuthor, into one single authors publications to see if the information belongs to same person or they are in fact different persons.

However, beside the effectiveness of the proposed method, ArnetMiner lacks the actual paper recommendation, specially based on the author's publications.

AN INTRODUCTION TO BATHAN

An earlier study (Teufel, S. and Moens, M 2002) showed that summarizing scientific papers needs a specific summarization method and other existing methods may not be a good fit. We showed in section [] that why an extractive summarization is a good fit for such aim. In this section, we ran an empirical study against Google scholar in terms of its ranking policy when it is highly based on their citation scores versus when they are ranked based on their textual similarities.

EMPIRICAL STUDY

In this study, we investigated ranking behavior of Google Scholar based on citation scores (by default) and based on textual similarity of papers. To produce similarity of papers, we extracted textual content of papers and applied stop-word removal to clean the plain text. We then counted the most frequent keyword of this bag of words and extracted textual portion of a paper within the occurrence of this most frequent keyword as a normal version of summary of a paper. In addition, we applied stemming after applying stop-word removal to group similar words under a *root word* as a family word. Afterwards, we counted frequency of words and selected most frequent keyword of a paper and produced summary of a paper based on same procedure for normal keywords. We used these two different versions of summaries in case if they result into different behavior.

Evaluation Metric

For the aim of this study, we evaluated Google scholar's ranking behavior based on *normality* and *regression curve estimation tests*.

Procedure

In order to evaluate ranking policy of Google scholar and observe effect of our proposal, we decided to select 8 random papers as input for Google scholar. Afterwards, we stored papers that Google scholar returned for each input paper for first 4 pages. We also stored citation scores of corresponding papers and their ranks in the Google scholar listing. On the other hand, we produced summaries of same papers based on aforementioned policies for both normal and stemmed keywords. Accordingly, we re-ranked Google scholar listings based on these two types of similarity and analyzed them based on evaluation metrics.

Similarities are produced based on cosine similarity which works in vector space. Common formula for cosine similarity can be illustrated as following:

$$\cos(\theta) = \frac{\sum_{i=1}^{n} A_i \times B_i}{\sqrt{\sum_{i=1}^{n} A_i^2} \times \sqrt{\sum_{i=1}^{n} B_i^2}} \tag{1}$$

Where $\sum_{i=1}^{n} A_i$ and $\sum_{i=1}^{n} B_i$ are the two summarized version of two given papers.

We used these similarities between candidate papers and input paper in order to generate a ranking list of similar papers.

Here, each of these vectors is representing a collection of words from each document that we want to make the similarity comparison.

Result

Accuracy and Distinctiveness of Similarity Values

In this section, we evaluated the similarity values produced based on our proposed mechanism. In first step, we applied *sample t-test* to find out if either similarity procedure produced significantly different sets of similarity values. According to P_{value} for all cases ($0.0 < P_{value} < 0.03$), we can conclude that similarity values produced by normal keywords are significantly different from those made by stemmed keywords.

For next step, we measured mean value of similarities of papers produced by either summary type. According to results, normal keywords would produce higher similarity values of papers ($19.48 < $ Mean value$_{normal\ keyword} < 24.25$) compared to similarity values produced by stemmed keywords ($13.27 < $ Mean value$_{stemmed\ keyword} < 19$).

Dependency of Ranking Policy of Google Scholar and Similarity Method to Citation Scores

In this section, we elaborated the feasibility of formulating ranking policy of Google scholar and summary-based method according to citation scores of returned papers. For this purpose, we considered citation score of a paper as an independent variable and a papers' rank as a dependent variable. To do so, we applied regression curve fitting tests and recorded results.

Results for summary-based method were not significant for any of the input papers for either type of keywords. On the other hand, we can summarize the results of curve fitting tests for Google scholar method as follows:

3rd, 4th and 8th input papers are associated with papers which followed a compound formula with common equation as *Rank=c*citation^t* where *c* is a constant and *t* is the regression coefficient and is different for each of these input papers. On the other hand, 7th input papers is linked with papers that can be formulated with a logistic regression formula with common equation

of $\frac{1}{u} + c * citation^t$ where *c*, *citation* and *t* are with same concept as before and *u* is the upper bound value for logistic regression. In addition, 1st, 2nd, 5th and 6th input papers are associated with papers which are bound with *inverse* *regression* with common formula as $Rank = \dfrac{t}{citation} + c$ with c, citation and t by same concepts as mentioned before.

In previous sections, we primarily showed that what the raw idea of a recommending scientific papers based on summaries of papers is and how it differs from other methods. In addition, we showed that how it differs to rank same documents if either summary-based method or citation scores are applied. In following sections, we aim to make our primary proposal for scholarly recommendation by giving detailed procedure on producing summary of papers and ranking them according to an input.

A JOURNEY TO SUMMARY-BASED RECOMMENDATION

To successfully recommend scientific papers based on their summaries, we first need to index paper repository. Accordingly, we need to establish mechanisms for building a candidate set of papers and ranking them.

Summary Production of Scholarly Documents

There are two major types of document summarization, i.e., abstractive summarization and extractive summarization. Abstractive summarization is done by internalizing the context and generating a list of keywords and keyphrases. These terms do not necessarily appear in the original document. On the other hand, extractive summarization is based on pulling out keywords and keyphrases directly from the original document.

Since our proposal considers similarity of papers based on textual similarity of papers, thus we do believe that relying on extractive summary will not result into accurate recommendation since terms produced in an abstractive summary may not appear within the content of original document.

Extractive summarization itself divides into different types based on their applications such as feature-based summarization (Vellino, A. 2009), latent semantic analysis (Gong, Y.and Liu, X. 2001), Bayesian topic model (Navarro, G.2001), topic clustering (Voorhees, E., M. (2000) and query-specific (Otterbacher, J et al. 2008).

For the purpose of paper recommendation, a feature-based method such as TF-IDF (Term Frequency- Inverse Document Frequency), most popular weighting method (Beel, J. et al. 2013, Beel, J. et al. 2015), would fit better as it considers the occurrences of original terms within the content of a document. Similarly, some prior works (Nascimento, C. et al. 2011, Sugiyama, K. and Kan, M. (2010)) have used TF over TF-IDF as in most cases there is not enough publications of an author to obtain an effective IDF value.

In a similar vein, we used TF value to build an extractive summary of a paper. This summary is produced on the basis of computing TF of terms within abstract and conclusion sections. Prior studies (Elkiss, A et al., 2008, Bradshaw, S., 2003) proved that abstract of a paper wouldn't be necessarily a comprehensive summary of corresponding paper.

We used unigrams over other variations based on a prior finding (Ledeneva, Y et al. 2008) where it showed that single words of a document are good representative of that corresponding document.

Policy for Producing a Set of Candidate Documents

Ledeneva et al. (2008) has showed that term frequencies (TF) are good weighting factors. Consequently, we used this idea for producing asset of candidate papers. To precisely decide how to use TF for this aim, we considered two facts:

1. Average length of sentences in a similar method which used raw TF in document summarization (without applying stop-word removing) is more than 18 terms (Kikuchi, Y. et al. 2015).
2. On the other hand, another study showed that using a set of stop words (containing 150 terms) reduced the average length of extracted sentences by about 20% (Christopher D. 2008).

Due to the fact that we have used a set of 600 terms for sto word removal, we decided to take into account 5 most frequent terms of each paper for the process of producing a set of candidate papers. To make it more accurate, we applied improved Kendall coefficient (Fagin, R. et al. 2003) to pick those papers with not only similar frequent keywords, but also with similar ranks of those frequent keywords.

Improved Kendall coefficient can be formulated in Equation 1:

$$K^{(p)}\left(\tau_1, \tau_2\right) = \sum_{\{i,j\} \in P(\tau_1, \tau_2)} \bar{K}_{i,j}^{(p)}\left(\tau_1, \tau_2\right) \tag{1}$$

Where τ_1 and τ_2 represent the two top K lists, i and j are items of τ_1 and τ_2 respectively, P is the set of unordered pairs of distinct elements and p indicated the penalty score for absence or misplace of *i* and *j* in either top lists. For computing K values, we would encounter either of the 4 following cases:

1. When both *i,j* appear in both top k lists, τ_1 and τ_2.
2. When both *i,j* appear in one top k list but only one of them appears in other top k list.
3. When *i* (or *j*) appears in one top k list and the other appears in another top k list.
4. When both *i,j* appear only in one top k list and neither appears in other top k list.

In case 1, if the order of *i,j* in τ_1 is opposite of τ_1's, then let $K^{(p)}(\tau_1,\tau_2)=1$. In case 2, if i(or j), is at higher rank of *j* (or *i*) in τ_1 and only *j* (or *i*) appears in τ_2, then let $K^{(p)}(\tau_1,\tau_2)=1$. In case 3, let $K^{(p)}(\tau_1,\tau_2)=1$. This is due to the intuition that when *i* is in τ_1, it is in higher rank of *j* in same list and when only j appears in τ_2, it means the order is opposite in other K list. Case 4 is a special case called Special pair. It is special because we do not know what penalty score we should give, 1 or 0. To solve this dilemma, there are 2 approaches, i.e., Optimistic approach when $p=0$ and Neutral approach when $p=\frac{1}{2}$. For our case, we made a new option as Pessimistic approach and assign a penalty score of $p=1$ for case 4.

Ranking Policy of Candidate Set

Levenshtein Edit Distance

Levenshtein edit distance or in short edit distance can be commonly defined as:

"The minimal number of insertions, deletions and substitutions to make two strings equal [55]."

In other words, the less value for an edit distance means that two strings are more similar compared to the situation that the edit distance is higher. This metric allows us to compare the similarity of two papers based on the least changes that is needed to be performed to make summaries of two papers equal.

Cosine Similarity

To rank the selected papers and for the purpose of this paper, the author also used cosine similarity. Cosine similarity applies in the Vector space model for string similarity computation. This function, computes the cosine of the angle between two vectors. To compute this angle, the function uses Dot product of two vectors. The two vectors here are two papers that we wish to measure their similarities.

The formula of cosine similarity can be demonstrated by Equation 2:

$$\cos\left(\theta\right) = \frac{\sum_{i=1}^{n} A_i \times B_i}{\sqrt{\sum_{i=1}^{n} A_i^2} \times \sqrt{\sum_{i=1}^{n} B_i^2}} \tag{2}$$

Where $\sum_{i=1}^{n} A_i$ and $\sum_{i=1}^{n} B_i$ are the two summarized version of two given papers. We use these similarities between candidate papers and input paper in order to generate a ranking list of similar papers.

EVALUATION

Setting and Dataset

For the purpose of this research work, the author decided to use data provided by DBLP[1]. DBLP provides an XML file (Ley, M. 2009) which allows users to crawl the data about papers and authors and venues. This XML file is publicly available and can be used to download papers based on the provided information per papers. This information is wrapped within several tags. The EE tag is responsible to contain the Digital object Identifier (DOI) of a paper.

To perform this offline evaluation, the author managed to retrieve publication records of different authors as a total of 3600 academic papers from ACM, IEEE, Springer, Elsevier and arXiv. To enrich this manually provided dataset, the author take advantages of the open dataset of ACL for this evaluation. The ACL Anthology Reference Corpus[2] is a frozen scholarly data set of publications in the field of computational linguistic. The data set consists of two versions with total number of more than 33000 scholarly papers. A part of data set consists of only PDF versions of papers while the rest of it has both PDF and raw textual format of each paper.

Data sets are accompanied with meta data of papers' general information such as the title and authors. Regarding failures of XML formats for some group of papers, we are able to include more than 35000 scientific papers, using ACL anthology reference corpus and the manually data set provided by crawling the data provided at the DBLP.

To prepare for the evaluation, the author creates two XML files for each paper of an author which first XML file conveys with the data that Bathan uses for Identifying knowledge and capturing relevant knowledge. These data are the five most frequent keywords of the paper and the summary produced from the designated portion of the paper. Second XML file is responsible to contain the stop-worded version of full-text of each paper. This version of each paper together with title and abstract will be used for building a comprehensive ground truth.. In section 6, the author brings a full discussion for this matter.

Ground Truth

The term qrels is coined by (Voorhees, E., M. 2000, 1998) which refers to the concatenation of judgment sets per topics for any given system. In our evaluation, each input paper can be seen as a topic and each of 4 different content-determined similarity techniques[3], can be seen as a judgment for that topic. Consequently, each paper has 15 qrels

$$\left(C_1^4 + C_2^4 + C_3^4 + C_4^4 = 4 = 6 = 4 = 1 = 15 \right)$$

that 4 of them $\left(C_1^4 \right)$ are special qrels, called original qrels which are directly produced by each judgment. Last but not least, there are two more qrels, namely union and intersection qrels.

The union qrels consists of documents that are considered relevant at least by one of the 4 judgments and the intersection qrels consists of documents that all judgments are agreed for its relevancy. Consequently, there are a total of 17 qrels. In the context of this evaluation, the union qrels and C_4^4 are equal and hence, there are a total number of 16 qrels to perform the evaluation.

Evaluation Metrics

Precision, Recall and F-measure

Precision, Recalls and F-measure are very common ways of measuring the throughput of recommender systems in IR-related topics. In general, precision shows how useful the system is and recall shows how accurate it is. Using F-measure, we can show a resultant of both precision and recall by using mean precision and mean recall.

Unanimously Retrieved Documents

Based on the findings from (Sauper, C et al. 2009), the author investigates the rank of relevant knowledge which is captured by Bathan with and without optimization. Principle of Unanimously ranked documents indicates that relevant document/knowledge is ranked in a higher position compared to the irrelevant one. Thus, a relevant document which contains a relevant knowledge should be placed at a higher position.

Skewness and Standard Deviation

By skewness we would like to compute noise within the similarity values that a particular system would return. Skewness is a way to investigate the symmetry of similarity values about the mean value. A negative value for skewness is obtained when values are left-skewed and it is positive when the values are right-skewed. A zero value for skewness, thus, means that the similarity values are perfectly symmetric about the mean .

Otherwise stated, the closer value of skewness to zero, the more normally distributed the observed similarity values. In this way, right-skewed means that the similarity values produced by a particular model tend to be higher than the mean and left-skewed is otherwise. Consequently, a high positive value for skewness is made when a particular system produces mainly values (finds articles) very similar to the input paper with a gap with the low values (articles with lower similarity) and otherwise for a high negative value for skewness.

The Standard deviation, commonly referred as Std. deviation, shows how spread out the observed values are from the mean value. Consequently, a low value for Std. deviation shows that data points are less spread out from the mean value and a high value of Std. is otherwise.

The value of skewness together with Standard deviation can effectively show us the correctness and effectiveness of the observed values.

Mutual Information

Intuitively, we expect a good recommender/classifier to retrieve actual document(s) within the predicted set. Consequently, one common metric to measure the correlation between the actual and predicted sets is to measure their mutual information (MI). Mutual information is a quantity that measures the relationship between two items to be co-occurred. Here, the mutual information would show the likelihood of returning relevant documents based on each qrels among first 30 results. The general formula for mutual information is shown as:

$$I\left(\mathrm{Pr};Ac\right) = \sum_{pr \in \mathrm{Pr}} \sum_{ac \in Ac} P\left(\mathrm{Pr}, Ac\right) * \log \frac{P\left(\mathrm{Pr}, Ac\right)}{P\left(\mathrm{Pr}\right) * P\left(Ac\right)} \tag{3}$$

Where P_r refers to the predicted results of a framework, A_c refers to the actual relevant documents which are listed by each qrels and $P(P_r; A_c)$ refers to the joint probability of predicted documents to be in the actual set.

Baseline

First Baseline

As Google and Microsoft have vertical search engines specifically developed for academic Web searching, a.k.a, Google scholar and Microsoft academic, we aim to implement baselines based on these two scholarly search engines.

To do as such, we took into the account the factors that Google and Microsoft use for recommending scholarly articles as followings:

- Author's h-index is a high-weighted metric in Google scholar
- In addition, recent researches show that the Google scholar puts high weight especially on citation scores and words occurring in the paper's title

- Moreover, to show the impact of future citations, we used Estimated citation counts provided by academic knowledge API

Second Baseline

In this evaluation, we considered analysis of retrieval behaviors for first 30 returned documents. Consequently, we decided to feed input papers to Google scholar and formulate the retrieval behavior of first 30 papers (first four pages) using regression curve estimation tests which provides us various tests for such aim.

To do as such, we formulated ranking policy of Google scholar for these papers based on the citation scores of papers as independent variable. Results are illustrated in Table. 1. Next, we used these equations and selected papers from our paper repository and ranked them according to the equation for each input paper in a descending order.

Table 1. Result of Regression Curve Fitting for Formulating Google Scholar Behavior Toward Each Input Paper.

Regression Curve	Formula	Input Paper
Linear	$Y=ax+c$	P_{22}, P_{14}
Logarithmic	$Y=a\ln(x)+c$	P_7, P_{19}, P_{30}
Compound	$Y=ca^x$	$P_2, P_{10}, P_{18}, P_{27}$
Exponential	$Y=ce^x$	P_8, P_{20}
Growth	$Y=e^{c+ax}$	P_9
Inverse	$Y = c + \dfrac{a}{x}$	$P_4, P_{12}, P_6, P_{23}, P_{25}, P_{28}$
Quadratic	$Y=c+a_1x+a_2x^2$	P_{16}
S	$Y = e^{c+\frac{a}{x}}$	P_{24}
Cubic	$Y=c+a_1x+a_2x^2+a_3x^3$	P_3, P_5, P_{13}

Y is the predicted rank of a paper

x is the citation score

c is the constant which stands for the similarity of title and abstract of a paper in repository with the input paper based on cosine similarity

a is the regression coefficient calculated based on the results of curve fitting tests.

Procedure

To conduct this evaluation, we randomly selected 30 papers from repository and fetched them one after another to the Bathan and baselines. For Bathan, we first populated a candidate set per input based on least K value and using aforementioned policies, we ranked selected papers and applied evaluation metrics to the ranked sets and observed the values.

In the case of first type of baseline, we computed h-index and Eh-index based on the provided data by Microsoft academic and examined same metrics on the retrieved lists produced by same ranking policies.

In the case of Google scholar, we assigned each input papers to the formula shown in Table. 5.1 based on the input's index. By knowing the similarity value of papers in the repository in terms of their abstract and title in respect to the input paper and their citation scores, we thus replace them with the c and x of their corresponding equation. The regression coefficient (a) is already known by the curve estimation tests for each input paper.

As a result, we can compute the value of Y1 for each paper in repository per input paper and extract the first 30 papers with the lowest value for Y and rank them in a descending order. Consequently, we apply same evaluation metrics on the retrieved lists for the further analysis.

Result

Precision, Recall and F1-Measure

Results of mean precision, recall and F1-measure for Bathan and baselines are shown in Table 2. From results we can see that although Google scholar performs more than two times better than Bathan and more than 5 times better than other two baselines in terms of precision, however its very low recall indicates that Google scholar returns a low proportion of relevant papers. This fact is better-shown with values of F1-measure where Bathan is 4 times better than Google scholar and twice better than other two baselines. Results of mean precision, recall and F1-measure for each ranking policies are shown in Table 3 and 4. From the results shown we can see that Bathan outperforms baselines for Cosine and Levenshtein ranking policies.

Table 2. Mean precision, recall and F1-measure of all 16 qrels in respect to 2 policies for Bathan and baselines

	Precision	Recall	F_1-measure
Bathan	0.068	0.038	0.048
Gogole Scholar (mimicked)	0.188	0.006	0.01
h-index	0.035	0.018	0.022
Eh-index	0.036	0.019	0.024

Table 3. Mean precision, recall and F1-measure of all 16 qrels for cosine similarity policy for Bathan and baselines

	Ranking Policy	Precision	Recall	F_1-measure
Bathan	Cosine	0.059	0.029	0.038
Gogole Scholar (mimicked)	Cosine	0.169	0.004	0.006
h-index	Cosine	0.037	0.017	0.023
Eh-index	Cosine	0.04	0.019	0.025

Table 4. Mean precision, recall and F1-measure of all 16 qrels for Levenshtein edit distance policy for Bathan and baselines

	Ranking Policy	Precision	Recall	F_1-measure
Bathan	Levenshtein	0.072	0.041	0.052
Gogole Scholar (mimicked)	Levenshtein	0.176	0.006	0.01
h-index	Levenshtein	0.033	0.0197	0.0246
Eh-index	Levenshtein	0.033	0.0199	0.0248

Skewness and Standard Deviation

Table 5 demonstrates results of skewness for similarity values for Bathan and baselines based on different methods of ranking. As we mentioned formerly, the value of Std. deviation and skewness together can show us a better understanding of closeness of similarity values to the mean. In other words, these values can predict the normality of observed values. As we can see from data shown in Table 5, both Std. deviation and skewness for Bathan for both ranking policies are far less than those for baselines. This means that Bathan not only returns more relevant papers (based on results for F1 measure) but also returned-papers are ordered based on their similarity with a steady pace from higher relevance to lower.

On the other hand, the high skewness and Std. deviation for baselines mean that papers at higher ranks are with huge differences in relevance compared to the lower ranks.

Table 5. Results of skewness for Bathan and baselines based on cosine similarity and Levenshtein edit distance policy. The skewness results together with the standard deviation results suggest that Bathan produces less spread out similarity values compared to the baselines for both ranking policies.

	Ranking Policy	Std. Deviation	Skewness
Bathan	Cosine	0.0305	-1.24
Gogole Scholar (mimicked)	Cosine	0.089	4.417
h-index	Cosine	2.102	1.511
Eh-index	Cosine	5.809	1.384
Bathan	Levenshtein	0.003	0.34
Gogole Scholar (mimicked)	Levenshtein	0.089	4.418
h-index	Levenshtein	3.116	2.284
Eh-index	Levenshtein	3.732	2.261

Unanimous Rank

Figure. 1,2, 3 and 4 demonstrates the distribution lines for all the 30 input papers based on the different ranking policies for Bathan and baselines. Research findings at[65,83] proves that unanimous documents are ranked in a higher position in the returned listing compared to the irrelevant documents. Having this in mind, we are using these charts to see that how frameworks used in our evaluation reacted to the input queries. By observing Figure. 1, we can see that in case of cosine ranking policy, Bathan ranks unanimous, or in other word relevant, documents as high as ranks below 7 and as low as 28 but most of relevant documents are ranked between 11 to 23. In case of Levenshtein ranking policy, unanimous documents are ranked between 5 to 26 but most relevant documents are ranked between 8 to 21. As a result, we can see that Levenshtein ranking policy improved the ranks of relevant documents for both the position and their frequencies.

Figure 1. Results of unanimous and others ranks of 16 qrels for input papers for Bathan based on ranking policies: Cosine similarity (Left) and Leveshtein edit distance (Right).

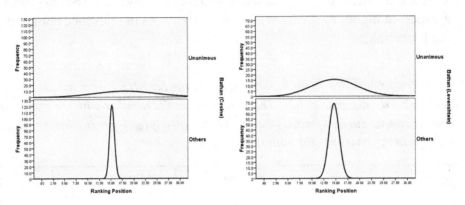

Figure 2. Results of unanimous and others ranks of 16 qrels for input papers for Google scholar (mimicked) based on ranking policies: Cosine similarity (Left) and Levenshtein edit distance (Right).

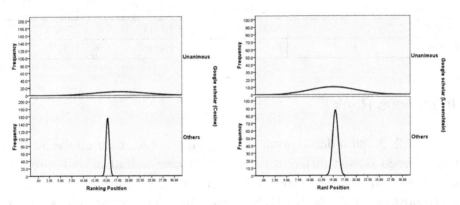

On the other hand, from Figure. 2 we can see that Google scholar ranks relevant documents between 9 to 26 for cosine ranking policy while most of relevant documents are positioned from 13 to 21. In case of Levenshtein ranking policy, relevant documents are placed from 6 to 24 with most document ranked at 11 to 21 with about same frequency. As we can see, Levenshtein ranking also improved ranks of relevant documents. As a comparison with Bathan, it has a better ranking for relevant documents for cosine policy (in terms of frequency of relevant documents in higher positions) and a worse ranking for relevant documents for Levenshtein policy.

Figure 3. Results of unanimous and others ranks of 16 qrels for input papers for baseline based on h-index based in respect to ranking policies: Cosine similarity (Left) and Levenshtein edit distance (Right)

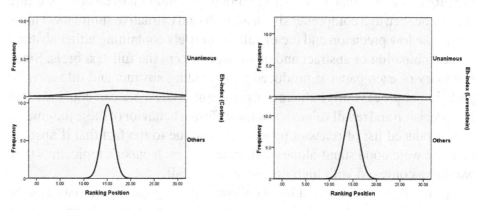

Figure 4. Results of unanimous and others ranks of 16 qrels for input papers for baseline based on Eh-index in respect to ranking policies: Cosine similarity (Left) and Levenshtein edit distance (Right)

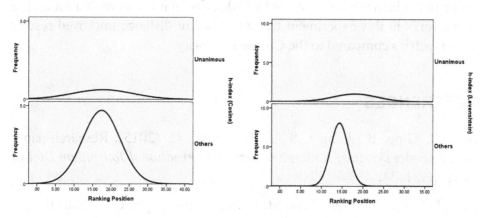

In addition, ranks of relevant and irrelevant documents for both cosine and Levenshtein ranking policies for baselines based on h-index and Eh-index are shown in Figure. 3 and 4. Although both baselines rank relevant documents in relatively good positions, but very low frequencies show that these two baselines find relevant documents way fewer often compared to Bathan and Google scholar. In a nutshell, Bathan responds better in Levenshtein policy compared to Google scholar while Google scholar responds better in Cosine policy.

CONCLUSION

We proved the fact that an abstract and/or a combination of abstract and title can not be seen as a comprehensive feature-based extractive summary. This is due to the low precision and recall values for qrels containing either abstract or a combination of abstract and other qrels except the full-text qrels. Since summary of each paper is produced by excluding abstract and title as valid parts in the process of producing papers' summaries, we can conclude that low precision and recall values show the different behavior of these judgments over produced list of relevant papers. That is due to the fact that if abstract and title were good stand-alone representees of each paper's topic, thus they would be conveyed with high precision and recall.

As a trail of previous finding, we showed that a paper's summary has the highest similarity with qrels that full-text qrels is a part of it. However, since the full-text comparison is time intensive [44] thus using Bathan would be a good replacement. For the choice of choosing a suitable ranking policy, we used Cosine similarity and Levenshtein edit distance. From results of our evaluation which we demonstrated and discussed, it is shown that for all the frameworks in this experiment Levenshtein edit distance improved results for all metrics compared to the Cosine similarity.

REFERENCES

Beel, J., Gipp, B., Langer, S., & Breitinger, C. (2015). Research-paper recommender systems: A literature survey. *International Journal on Digital Libraries*, 1–34.

Beel, J., Langer, S., Genzmehr, M., Gipp, B., Breitinger, C., & Nürnberger, A. (2013). Research paper recommender system evaluation: A quantitative literature survey. *Proceedings of the International Workshop on Reproducibility and Replication in Recommender Systems Evaluation, RepSys '13*, 15–22.

Bogers, T., & van den Bosch, A. (2008). Recommending scienti_c articles using citeulike. *Proceedings of the 2008 ACM Conference on Recommender Systems, RecSys '08*, 287-290. 10.1145/1454008.1454053

Bradshaw, S. (2003). Reference directed indexing: Redeeming relevance for subject search in citation indexes. Lecture Notes in Computer Science, 2769, 499–510.

Christopher, D. (2008). *Introduction to information retrieval.* Cambridge University Press.

Elkiss, A., Shen, S., Fader, A., Erkan, G., States, D., & Radev, D. (2008). Blind men and elephants: What do citation summaries tell us about a research article? *Journal of the American Society for Information Science and Technology, 59*(1), 51–62. doi:10.1002/asi.20707

Fagin, R., Kumar, R., & Sivakumar, D. (2003). Comparing top k lists. *Proceedings of the Fourteenth Annual ACM-SIAM Symposium on Discrete Algorithms, SODA '03*, 28–36.

Gong, Y., & Liu, X. (2001). Generic text summarization using relevance measure and latent semantic analysis. *Proceedings of the 24th Annual International ACM SIGIR Conference on Research and Development in Information Retrieval, SIGIR '01*, 19–25. 10.1145/383952.383955

Good, N., Schafer, J. B., Konstan, J. A., Borchers, A., Sarwar, B., Herlocker, J., & Riedl, J. (1999). Combining collaborative filtering with personal agents for better recommendations. *Proceedings of the Sixteenth National Conference on Artificial Intelligence and the Eleventh Innovative Applications of Artificial Intelligence Conference Innovative Applications of Artificial Intelligence, AAAI '99/IAAI '99*, 439-446.

He, Q., Pei, J., Kifer, D., Mitra, P., & Giles, L. (2010). Context-aware citation recommendation. *Proceedings of the 19th International Conference on World Wide Web, WWW '10*, 421-430. 10.1145/1772690.1772734

Hong, K., Jeon, H., & Jeon, C. (2013a). Advanced personalized research paper recommendation system based on expanded userprofile through semantic analysis. *International Journal of Digital Content Technology and its Applications, 7*(15), 67-76.

Hong, K., Jeon, H., & Jeon, C. (2013b). Personalized research paper recommendation system using keyword extraction based on userprofile. *Journal of Convergence Information Technology, 8*(16), 106-116.

Hyland, K. (2003). Self-citation and self-reference: Credibility and promotion in academic publication. *Journal of the American Society for Information Science, 54*, 251259.

Kikuchi, Y., Hirao, T., Takamura, H., Okumura, M., & Nagata, M. (2015) Summarizing a Document by Trimming a Nested Tree Structure. *Journal of Natural Language Processing.*

Ledeneva, Y., Gelbukh, A., & García-Hernández, R. A. (2008) Terms Derived from Frequent Sequences for Extractive Text Summarization. In *9th International Conference on Intelligent Text Processing and Computational Linguistics: CICLing 2008*, (pp. 593-604). Springer Berlin Heidelberg.

Ley, M. (2009). Dblp: Some lessons learned. *Proc. VLDB Endow., 2*(2), 1493–1500. doi: 10.14778/1687553.1687577

Ma. N, Guan, J., & Zhao, Y. (2008). Bringing pagerank to the citation analysis. *Inf. Process. Manage., 44*(2), 800-810.

Merton, R. K. (1986). The Matthew Effect in Science. *Science, 159*(3810), 56–63. doi:10.1126cience.159.3810.56 PMID:5634379

Nascimento, C., Laender, A. H., da Silva, A. S., & Gonçalves, M. A. (2011). A source independent framework for research paper recommendation. *Proceedings of the 11th Annual International ACM/IEEE Joint Conference on Digital Libraries, JCDL '11*, 297–306. 10.1145/1998076.1998132

Navarro, G. (2001). A guided tour to approximate string matching. *ACM Computing Surveys, 33*(1), 31–88. doi:10.1145/375360.375365

Nykl, M., Jezek, K., Fiala, D., & Dostal, M. (2014). PageRank variants in the evaluation of citation networks. *Journal of Informetrics, 8*(3), 683–692. doi:10.1016/j.joi.2014.06.005

Otterbacher, J., Erkan, G., & Radev, D., R. (2008). Biased lexrank: Passage retrieval using random walks with question-based priors. *Inf. Process. Manage., 45*(1), 42–54. doi:.2008.06.004 doi:10.1016/j.ipm

Pohl, S., Radlinski, F., & Joachims, T. (2007). Recommending related papers based on digital library access records. *Proceedings of the 7th ACM/IEEE-CS Joint Conference on Digital Libraries*, 417-418.

Rijsbergen, C. J. V. (1979). *Information Retrieval* (2nd ed.). Butterworth-Heinemann.

Sauper, C., & Barzilay, R. (2009). *Automatically generating wikipedia articles: A structure-aware approach.* Academic Press.

Stanovich, K. E. (1986). Matthew effects in reading: Some consequences of individual differences in the acquisition of literacy. *Reading Research Quarterly, 22*, 1986.

Sugiyama, K., & Kan, M. (2010). Scholarly paper recommendation via user's recent research interests. *Proceedings of the 2010 Joint International Conference on Digital Libraries, JCDL 2010*, 29–38. 10.1145/1816123.1816129

Tagliacozzo, R. (1977). Self citations in scientific literature. *The Journal of Documentation, 33*(4), 251–265. doi:10.1108/eb026644

Teufel, S., & Moens, M. (2002, December). Summarizing scientific articles: Experiments with relevance and rhetorical status. *Computational Linguistics, 28*(4), 409–445. doi:10.1162/089120102762671936

Vellino, A. (2009). Recommending journal articles with pagerank ratings. Recommender Systems 2009.

Vellino, A. (2010). A comparison between usage-based and citation-based methods for recommending scholarly research articles. *Proceedings of the American Society for Information Science and Technology, 47*(1), 1-2. 10.1002/meet.14504701330

Voorhees, E. M. (1998). Variations in relevance judgments and the measurement of retrieval effectiveness. In *Information Processing and Management* (pp. 315–323). ACM Press.

Voorhees, E. M. (2000). Variations in relevance judgments and the measurement of retrieval effectiveness. *Information Processing & Management, 36*(5), 697–716. doi:10.1016/S0306-4573(00)00010-8

ENDNOTES

1   https://dblp.uni-trier.de/
2   https://acl-arc.comp.nus.edu.sg/
3   These are similarities based on the documents title, abstract, title-abstract and full-text.

Chapter 6

Enhancing Academic Recommendation Regarding Common Coauthors' Publication Records

ABSTRACT

In this chapter, the authors investigated the feasibility of any improvement in paper recommendation by recommending similar papers to an input paper from the publication record of the first author. Although there are numerous approaches for recommending academic papers, they did not consider intellectually recommending papers based on the publication record of common coauthors. Consequently, they are motivated to introduce a remedy for this shortcoming by recommending scholarly papers based on similarity of textual references to visual features which considers the similarity of text fragments of one's publication record to any of their visual features (i.e., tables and figures). Based on the results of evaluation, the proposed enhancement will increase the mean precision, recall, and accordingly, the F-measure. In addition, it increases the position of the relevant papers in the returned list of documents.

DOI: 10.4018/978-1-7998-0961-6.ch006

INTRODUCTION

The growing amount of researching tasks on the Web makes it necessary to be accurate in the terms of recommending correct documents upon a user's query. For this matter, there are numerous approaches proposed to tackle this dilemma. Methods which use citation scores, a full-text approach, using coauthor networks etc. are some examples of such systems. Nevertheless, each of these techniques suffer from one or more critical issues which we highlighted them in our previous works (Alli, 2015; Alli et.al., 2015) and proposed solutions for them.

Previously (Alli, 2015) we introduced a summary-based method which takes into account an extractive summary of papers in order to recommend relevant papers to an input paper. Moreover, we proposed a novel way to investigate similar papers from one's publication record. We call this method; *similarity of textual references to visual features (Alli, 2015)* as it takes into account the similarity of fragment texts that are referring to any visual element of appear such as tables and figures.

The motivation behind such work is due to the fact that there is no existing method which intellectually recommends papers from -at least- first author of an input paper. We do believe that using proposed method, hence we can benefit users with a better quality in recommendation.

The primary goal of this paper is to illustrate the effectiveness of this method on the retrieval behavior for recommending scientific paper.

RELATED WORK

Using Collaborative and Content-Based Filtering in a Digital Library

(A.Vellino 2009) suggested a collaborative system to recommend research papers for producing numerical rating rather boolean rating that TechLens+ (R. Torres et.al 2004) produces. Therefore, they use Page Rank values in their algorithm. The expectation of the result was to enhance the recommendation results for research papers. However, the author of the paper mentioned that the evaluation results shown that Page Rank values notably decreased the quality of recommendation.

Docear's (J.Beel et.al 2013) is suggested as a research paper recommender which uses a content-based filtering (CBF) approach over its digital library. This recommender requires users to build a mind map for the system in order to enrich the information repository of the recommender[1] and using this mind map together by applying various CBF techniques, therefore the system retrieves a list of related papers.

CiteULike (T. Bogers et.al 2008) is a search engine that applies two collaborative filtering (CF) algorithms, called user-based filtering and item-based filtering where in former, the system tries to match the active user with neighboring users and in latter, filtering is done by finding neighboring similar items.

In general, a CF recommender hardly reaches to the expected performance when the number of users is small. Moreover, it has been shown (Liang, T.-P et.al 2008, Bogers, T. et.al 2009) that a CBF recommender performs better than a CF recommender.

Using Citation Scores

(B.Gipp et.al 2009) has made effort to improve the classical keyword-based searching by introducing a hybrid recommender system which uses more factors for document preference such as citation analysis, author analysis, source analysis, implicit ratings and explicit ratings. Therefore, the recommender accepts six inputs, i.e., text, references, authors, sources, ratings and documents which at least one of them must be provided by the user. Accordingly, using these inputs, the proposed system will provide users with a list of relevant papers. The main drawback of this system is the user engagement for recommendation.

A Co-training approach (C. Caragea et.al 2015) is suggested for topic classification based on the citation and text of a research paper. The main task of proposed approach is to classify papers that are bound in a citation network. To evaluate the performance of corresponding system, authors of the paper categorized their dataset into 5 groups, i.e., AI, IR, DB, ML and HCI. Accordingly, using text and citation information of each paper they evaluated their system.

Although this work does not explicitly targets the paper recommendation, but classified papers can enhance the recommendation. By considering this, the evaluation over their data set shows that AI topic is the hardest to be classified for being too general and having few instances[2] in the data set. These two cons greatly affect the usage of such system.

Applying Coauthor Network

Using coauthor network for predicting similarity of authors can be divided into 3 techniques:

A coauthor similarity system (S.Han et.al 2013, Y.Sun et.al 2011) is where the system tries to find similarities between users' and authors' interests according to their research concerns. Such system may or may not recommend papers based on this similarity, however, in case of recommendation, the system will retrieve many irrelevant papers especially when predicted authors are working on a wide range of topics.

Recommendation Based on the User's Interest

(K. Sugiyama et al 2010) introduced a key-phrase based system to recommend papers based on the users' interests by considering his/her other publication records. To do such, the proposed system builds up a user profile of researchers based on their publication record as either senior2 or junior3 researchers.

As this is mentioned, this system requires additional data for producing users' profile. Moreover, such system has even a much bigger problem. If we rely solely on someone's publication, there is no necessity for someone to narrow down his/her researching field to one or few topics. It is common that someone changes its working direction after an accomplishment or achievement. Authors has mentioned that they would put more weight (near to 1) for recent papers and less weight (near to 0) for older papers to fix this issue. Nonetheless, this is still possible that an author is already finished its work with some recent publication and has started a new topic.

AN OVERVIEW OF THE SUMMARY-BASED APPROACH

As we mentioned previously, the aim of this chapter is to investigate the feasibility of using publication record of the first author of the input paper in order to improve the quality of recommended papers. To do as such, we use our previously introduced summary-based recommender as the baseline. As we described this recommender in chapter 5, summary-based recommender uses an extractive summary of each paper in order to return relevant papers. To make an extractive summary of a paper, there are different techniques such as feature-based approaches. One of the most common feature-based approache is to use TF-IDF for creating the summary of a document. There are some prior works (C. Nascimento et.al 2011, F. Ferrara, et.al 2011, K. Sugiyama et al 2010) which use a raw TF as it fitted to their problem. Similarly, to make an extractive summary we use the raw TF as well. This TF value is computed after extracting the textual part of each paper after abstract section (Excluding abstract) until before the conclusion. As a recall, we bring a short description of this recommender here for the purpose of clarity.

Paper Summary Production

To produce the summary, we decide to choose the first 5 most frequent keywords of each paper as a measurement for selecting candidate papers as well as the first most frequent keyword will be used for paper summary production.

One might argue that there are abstracts for each paper that can be seen as a relevant summary of a scientific paper. However, this has been proven (A. Elkiss et.al 2008) that the abstract of a paper is not sufficient to be considered as a comprehensive summary of the whole paper so that an abstract of a paper cannot be used for this matter. In addition, it is shown (S. Ye, et.al 2007) that keywords with high frequencies are more probable to be co-occurred within a passage. Moreover, according to the Zipf's law (D. M. W. Powers 1998) the frequency of a keyword in a corpus has inverse relation to its rank. This can be shown mathematically as $cf_i \propto \frac{1}{i}$ where cf_i indicates the frequency of a keyword with rank i.

As a result, the 5th most frequent keyword is expected to have an occurrence ratio of 1:5 regarding to the most frequent keyword. For a short type of corpus like scientific papers, we do believe that storing the first 5 most frequent keywords will be sufficient for containing an overview of each paper for the purpose of candidate paper selection.

Candidate Papers Selection and Ranking Policies

Candidate Paper Selection Policy

We believe that papers with high frequent keywords are more likely to be similar in the content. To make this concept even more accurate, we decided to take into account the rank of those frequent keywords as well. By indexing the paper repository based on their 5 most frequent keywords, whenever there is an input paper, we compare its frequent keywords with all the other papers and select all those papers that have at least one common frequent keyword with input paper. Accordingly, using improved Kendall coefficient (R. Fagin et.al 2003), we are able to find first 30 papers3which are with least K values compare to the rest of papers.

Improved Kendall coefficient can be formulated in Equation 1:

$$K^{(p)}\left(\tau_1, \tau_2\right) = \sum_{\{i,j\} \in P\left(\tau_1, \tau_2\right)} \bar{K}_{i,j}^{(p)}\left(\tau_1, \tau_2\right) \tag{1}$$

Where τ_1 and τ_2 represent the two top K lists, i and j are items of τ_1 and τ_2 respectively, P is the set of unordered pairs of distinct elements and p indicated the penalty score for absence or misplace of i and j in either top lists. For computing K values, we would encounter either of the 4 following cases:

1. When both *i,j* appear in both top k lists, τ_1 and τ_2.
2. When both *i,j* appear in one top k list but only one of them appears in other top k list.
3. When *i* (or *j*) appears in one top k list and the other appears in another top k list.
4. When both *i,j* appear only in one top k list and neither appears in other top k list.

In case 1, if the order of *i,j* in τ_1 is opposite of τ_1's, then let $K^{(p)}(\tau_1,\tau_2)=1$. In case 2, if i(or j), is at higher rank of *j* (or *i*) in τ_1 and only *j* (or *i*) appears in τ_2, then let $K^{(p)}(\tau_1,\tau_2)=1$. In case 3, let $K^{(p)}(\tau_1,\tau_2)=1$. This is due to the intuition that when *i* is in τ_1, it is in higher rank of *j* in same list and when only j appears in τ_2, it means the order is opposite in other K list. Case 4 is a special case called Special pair. It is special because we do not know what penalty score we should give, 1 or 0. To solve this dilemma, there are 2 approaches, i.e., Optimistic approach when $p=0$ and Neutral approach when $p = \frac{1}{2}$. For our case, we made a new option as Pessimistic approach and assign a penalty score of $p=1$ for case 4.

Ranking Policy

Although the originally we introduced the summary-based method with two different ranking policies, i.e., *Levenshtein edit distance* and *Cosine similarity*, but for the sake of this paper we only consider the results of this recommender based on the Cosine similarity and its improvement(s) based on the proposed improvement.

Cosine similarity applies in the Vector space model for sting similarity computation. This function, computes the cosine of the angle between two vectors. To compute this angle, the function uses Dot product of two vectors. The two vectors here are two papers that we wish to measure their similarities.

The formula of cosine similarity can be demonstrated by Equation 2:

$$\cos\left(\theta\right) = \frac{\sum_{i=1}^{n} A_i \times B_i}{\sqrt{\sum_{i=1}^{n} A_i^2} \times \sqrt{\sum_{i=1}^{n} B_i^2}} \tag{2}$$

Where $\sum_{i=1}^{n} A_i$ and $\sum_{i=1}^{n} B_i$ are the two summarized version of two given papers. We use these similarities between candidate papers and input paper in order to generate a ranking list of similar papers.

AN OVERVIEW OF THE PROPOSED OPTIMIZATION

Although there are numerous techniques which are developed to recommend scientific papers upon an input paper, nevertheless neither of them intellectually recommends papers from the publication record of –at least- first author of the input paper. That motivates us to take into consideration of developing such framework. We call this technique similarity of textual references to visual features where the similarity of one's paper is calculated based on the similarity of text fragments of the papers' content that refer to any visual element(s) of that paper.

The concept of visuality here is any visual elements, i.e., table and figures that are commonly used by authors to describe their proposed framework and/or the result of their experiments. Due to the fact that similar works of coauthors are focused on solving similar problems as well as developing and improving similar techniques, we realized that comparing these visual factors among their published researches will be a great help for finding similar works of those authors.

EVALUATION

Settings and Data Set Configurations

To evaluate the effectiveness of proposed improvement over the baseline, we decide to perform an evaluation over a data set of scientific papers in the field of computer science and technology. To prepare for this, we use the data provided by DBLP[4]. DBLP provides an XML file (M. Ley 2009) which allows users to crawl the data about papers and authors and venues. Each XML records in this XML file indicates a unique paper with several information regarding to it. This information is wrapped within several tags. The EE tag demonstrates the Digital object Identifier (DOI) of a paper. We use this DOI to download[5] needed papers to perform an offline experiment. Besides DOI, each paper has one or more author tags, one title tag and one year tag which indicates the publication year of the paper There are few other tags that are not of our interests.

To perform our offline experiment successfully, we established to extract publication records of different authors. To do such, we extracted authors information from the XML file and accordingly, we crawl this XML file in order to obtain the author, title, EE and year tags. Thereafter, we create an XML file for each author which consists information of his/her publication records. Using the content of EE tag, therefore, we can request and download authors' papers.

Next, we create two other XML files for each paper of an author which in first XML file we store data that are necessary for the summary-based to work with and in second XML file we store the stop-worded version of full-text of each paper. We use this full version together with title and abstract information of each paper in order to build a set of relevant sets. In section 6.4.1, we will discuss this in more details.

Difficulties and Shortcomings

To provide a repository of authors and their corresponding papers to perform the offline experiment, we have to extract the pdf link for each paper from its DOI. For the fact that there are quite a huge amount of different journals and digital libraries, we only choose to set our system to download papers from ACM, IEEE, Springer, Elsevier, arXiv, Siam and wiley. For Siam and wiley journals and papers, we had the difficulty of setting cookies and accessing the online pdf. For ACM and Springer we had some problem during crawling papers where ACM digital library returns a 403 forbidden HTTP status code from time to time, meaning that the server refuses to give access to open the pdf link. That is probably for blocking robots from crawling ACM digital library and for Springer library, there were times that the connection reaches a read time out exception for no reason. To access papers from IEEE digital libraries, we were not able to save the paper's title.

To sum it up, we managed to download more than 7500 papers from ACM, IEEE, Springet, Elsevier and arXiv using institutional rights.

Improvement of Data Set Collection

Considering the aforementioned difficulties, we take using the open data set of ACL into account for our experiment. The ACL Anthology Reference Corpus[6] is a frozen scholarly data set of publications in the field of computational linguistic. The data set consists of two versions with total number of more than 33000 scholarly papers. A part of data set consists of only PDF versions of papers while the rest of it has both PDF and raw textual format of each paper.

Data sets are accompanied with meta data of papers' general information such as the title and authors. Since baselines of this evaluation are dependent to the authors' h-index and estimated h-index, we considered fist author of each paper as the corresponding author responsible for the computation of h-index and estimated h-index of those papers.

Regarding failures of XML formats for some group of papers, we are able to include more than 35000 scientific papers, using ACL anthology reference corpus and the manually data set provided by crawling the data provided at the DBLP.

Evaluation Metrics

In this section, we will go through the metrics that we use to evaluate our system.

Precision, Recall and F-Score Based on Query-Relevance Set (Qrels)

Precision, Recalls and F-score are very common ways of measuring the throughput of a recommender systems in IR-related topics.

In general, precision shows how useful the system is and recall shows how accurate it is. Using F-score, we can show a resultant of both precision and recall by using mean precision and mean recall.

For the fact that there is no ground truth available for the context of this research and this does not look feasible to ask users to go through thousands of papers and select relevant papers from the paper repository, hence we decided to use query relevance sets or in short, qrels to obtain a ground truth.

The term qrels is coined by (E.M Voorhees 2000, 1998) which refers to the concatenation of judgment sets per topics for any given system. In our evaluation, each input paper can be seen as a topic and each of 4 different content-determined similarity techniques[7], beside our summary method, can be seen as a judgment for that topic. Consequently, each paper has 15 qrels

$$\left(C_1^4 + C_2^4 + C_3^4 + C_4^4 = 4 = 6 = 4 = 1 = 15 \right)$$

that 4 of them $\left(C_1^4 \right)$ are special qrels, called original qrels which are directly produced by each judgment. Last but not least, there are two more qrels, namely union and intersection qrels.

The union qrels consists of documents that are considered relevant at least by one of the 4 judgments and the intersection qrels consists of documents that all judgments are agreed for its relevancy. Consequently, we have 17 qrels. In our scenario, the union qrels and C_4^4 are equal and hence, we have a total number of 16 qrels to perform the evaluation.

Unanimously Retrieved Documents

Based on the findings from (C. Sauper et.al 2009), we can interrogate the feasibility of unanimous ranks of relevant documents for any particular recommender. This principle indicates that same or unanimously judged documents for different judgments are usually ranked before those documents that are not unanimously judged. Based on our evaluation setting, we can use this principle in order to show that which system puts relevant documents in a higher position compare to the irrelevant documents.

Procedure

We randomly selected 30 papers from 30 different authors. 15 of authors have publication record less than 10 and the other 15 authors have more than 10 publications, based on our paper repository. We considered the size of authors' publication to make sure that the effect will be applicable for authors with large and small publication record.

Once we retrieve similar papers according to the summary-based approach and once we considered the similarity of textual references to the visual features for the publication record of first author of each input paper. Using the ground truth and evaluation metrics from section, we recorded the results of each case for the further analysis on the effectiveness of intellectually retrieving similar papers from ones publication record.

Therefore, to be able to measure the feasibility of effectiveness of such technique to the efficiency of the summary-based recommendation, we added 10% of the size of retrieval (3 papers) from the papers that are considered similar according to their similarity of textual references to visual features and added them at the top of the list. It is due to the intuition that common coauthors will work on similar type of papers.

EVALUATION RESULTS

Results of Precision, Recall and F-measure Based on qrels

The results of average mean precision, recall and F-measure for the summary-based with and without consideration toward the publication record of first

Table 1. Average mean precision, recall and F-measure for Cosine ranking policies for Bathan with and without consideration toward the publication record of the first author of input paper, for all 16 qrels.

	With Optimization	Ranking Policy	Precision	Recall	F-measure
Bathan	Yes	Cosine Similarity	0.036	0.019	0.025
Bathan	No	Cosine Similarity	0.017	0.008	0.01

author of the input paper for all the 16 qurls is shown at the Table 1. According to the results, we can see that using the similarity of textual references to visual features will improve the results by more than 200%. We can also break down the results based on each qrels. The results for each 16 qrels for with and without consideration toward the proposed improvement can be illustrated in the Table 2.

From the results of precision and recall for each qrels, we can see that using the proposed improvement will return papers based on the original title qrels while in normal case, the system fails to return any relevant documents for that judgment. In addition, the result of precision and recall -and accordingly, F-measure- for all the 16 qrels is improved by applying the improvement to the summary-based retrieval strategy.

Unanimous Ranks

The results of unanimous ranks for with and without consideration toward publication record are illustrated in Table 3. From the performance results we can see that the mean rank of relevant documents was improved by a little bit more than 4 positions.

The break-down of the results for each 16 qrels is shown in Table 4. From the results for each 16 qrels we can see that except for the original Full qrel, the summary-based without any improvement would rank relevant documents in a lower position compared with the time that the improvement is applied.

In addition, we can see that for the ranks produced by the introduced improvement, the original title qrels has the best mean rank (7:00) followed by other qrels that are a combination of title judgment. This means that similarity of textual references to visual features from one's publication has a direct binding with the title similarity of others' publications

Table 2. Comparision of the results of precision and recall of 16 qrels based on Cosine ranking policy for Bathan with and without introduced improvement.

qrel Type	Ranking Policy	Precision Without Optimization	Recall Without Optimization	Precision With Optimization	Recall With Optimization
Intersection qrels	Cosine similarity	0.000	0.000	0.000	0.000
Full (original qrel)	Cosine similarity	0.016	0.016	0.033	0.033
Title (original qrel)	Cosine similarity	0.000	0.000	0.033	0.033
Abstract (original qrel)	Cosine similarity	0.011	0.011	0.033	0.033
Title and abstract (original qrel)	Cosine similarity	0.011	0.25	0.033	0.055
Full-Title	Cosine similarity	0.016	0.008	0.033	0.016
Full-Abstract	Cosine similarity	0.025	0.012	0.044	0.022
Full-Title and abstract	Cosine similarity	0.02	0.013	0.033	0.021
Title-Abstract	Cosine similarity	0.011	0.005	0.033	0.016
Title-Title and abstract	Cosine similarity	0.011	0.007	0.033	0.019
Abstract-Title and Abstract	Cosine similarity	0.016	0.011	0.033	0.025
Full-Title and abstract	Cosine similarity	0.025	0.008	0.041	0.014
Full-Title-Title and abstract	Cosine similarity	0.02	0.006	0.033	0.012
Full-Abstract-Title and abstract	Cosine similarity	0.026	0.010	0.041	0.017
Title-Abstract-Title and abstract	Cosine similarity	0.016	0.006	0.033	0.014
All (Union qrels)	Cosine similarity	0.026	0.007	0.04	0.011
Mean	Cosine similarity	0.017	0.01	0.036	0.02

Table 3. Comparision of the results of Mean Unanimous ranks of 16 qrels based on Cosine ranking policy for Bathan with and without introduced improvement.

qrel Type	Ranking Policy	Mean Unanimous Rank Without Optimization	Mean Unanimous Rank With Optimization
Intersection qrels	Cosine similarity	0.000	0.000
Full (original qrel)	Cosine similarity	27.00	27.5
Title (original qrel)	Cosine similarity	0.000	7.00
Abstract (original qrel)	Cosine similarity	13.00	11.5
Title and abstract (original qrel)	Cosine similarity	15.00	13.00
Full-Title	Cosine similarity	27.00	20.66
Full-Abstract	Cosine similarity	23.5	19.00
Full-Title and abstract	Cosine similarity	23.00	20.25
Title-Abstract	Cosine similarity	13.00	10.00
Title-Title and abstract	Cosine similarity	15.00	11.00
Abstract-Title and Abstract	Cosine similarity	14.00	13.33
Full-Title and abstract	Cosine similarity	23.5	16.00
Full-Title-Title and abstract	Cosine similarity	23.00	17.6
Full-Abstract-Title and abstract	Cosine similarity	20.66	18.5
Title-Abstract-Title and abstract	Cosine similarity	14.00	11.75
All (Union qrels)	Cosine similarity	20.66	16.2
Mean	Cosine similarity	20.57	16.00

CONCLUSION

In this chapter, we investigated the possibility of improvements on the paper recommendation based on the intellectually recommending papers from the publication record of the first author of an input paper. We call this method;

Table 4. Comparision of the results of precision and recall of 16 qrels based on Cosine ranking policy for Bathan with and without introduced improvement.

	With Optimization	Ranking Policy	Mean Unanimous Ranks
Bathan	Yes	Cosine Similarity	16.00
Bathan	No	Cosine Similarity	20.57

similarity of textual references to visual features, at it uses the part of textual content of a paper that refers to its visual elements, i.e., tables and figures. To interrogate any positive effect of such method, we used our previously implemented method as a baseline. This baseline uses an extractive summary of each paper as a reperesntive model of that corresponding paper in order to find relevant papers. Our performance results based on the mean precision, recall, F-measure and unanimous ranks shows that using the proposed improvement will increase the precision and recall by 200% and F-measure by 250% as well as it ranks relevant papers by more than 4 positions higher than the baseline.

REFERENCES

Alli, M. (2015). Similarity prediction based on the similarity of textual references to visual features. *Proceedings of the 7th International Joint Conference on Knowledge Discovery, Knowledge Engineering and Knowledge Management*, 637–643. 10.5220/0005629006370643

Alli, M., Alli, V., & Feng, L. (2015). Papers' similarity based on the summarization merits. *Behavioral, Economic and Socio-cultural Computing (BESC), 2015 International Conference on*, 137–142. doi:10.1109/BESC.2015.7365971

Beel, J., Langer, S., Genzmehr, M., & Nürnberger, A. (2013). Introducing docear's research paper recommender system. In *Proceedings of the 13th ACM/IEEE-CS Joint Conference on Digital Libraries, JCDL '13*. ACM. 10.1145/2467696.2467786

Bogers, T., & van den Bosch, A. (2008). Recommending scientific articles using citeulike. *Proceedings of the 2008 ACM Conference on Recommender Systems, RecSys '08*, 287–290. 10.1145/1454008.1454053

Bogers, T., & van den Bosch, A. (2009). *Collaborative and content-based filtering for item recommendation on social bookmarking websites.* Academic Press.

Caragea, C., Bulgarov, F. A., & Mihalcea, R. (2015). Co-training for topic classification of scholarly data. *Proceedings of the 2015 Conference on Empirical Methods in Natural Language Processing, EMNLP 2015,* 2357–2366. 10.18653/v1/D15-1283

Elkiss, A., Shen, S., Fader, A., Erkan, G., States, D., & Radev, D. (2008, January). Radev. Blind men and elephants: What do citation summaries tell us about a research article? *Journal of the American Society for Information Science and Technology, 59*(1), 51–62. doi:10.1002/asi.20707

Fagin, R., Kumar, R., & Sivakumar, D. (2003). Comparing top k lists. *Proceedings of the Fourteenth Annual ACM-SIAM Symposium on Discrete Algorithms, SODA '03,* 28–36.

Ferrara, F., Pudota, N., & Tasso, C. (2011). A keyphrase-based paper recommender system. *Communications in Computer and Information Science, 249,* 14–25. doi:10.1007/978-3-642-27302-5_2

Gipp, B., Beel, J., & Hentschel, C. S. (2009). A research paper recommender system. *Proceedings of the International Conference on Emerging Trends in Computing.*

Han, S., He, D., Brusilovsky, P., & Yue, Z. (2013). Coauthor prediction for junior researchers. In Social Computing, Behavioral-Cultural Modeling and Prediction, volume 7812 of Lecture Notes in Computer Science, (pp. 274–283). Springer Berlin Heidelberg. doi:10.1007/978-3-642-37210-0_30

Ley, M. (2009). Dblp: Some lessons learned. *Proc. VLDB Endow., 2*(2), 1493–1500. doi: 10.14778/1687553.1687577

Liang, T.-P., Yang, Y.-F., Chen, D.-N., & Ku, Y.-C. (2008). A semantic expansion approach to personalized knowledge recommendation. *Decision Support Systems, 45*(3), 401–412. doi:10.1016/j.dss.2007.05.004

Nascimento, C., Laender, A. H., da Silva, A. S., & Gonçalves, M. A. (2011). A source independent framework for research paper recommendation. *Proceedings of the 11th Annual International ACM/IEEE Joint Conference on Digital Libraries, JCDL '11,* 297–306. 10.1145/1998076.1998132

Powers, D. M. W. (1998). Applications and explanations of zipf's law. *Proceedings of the Joint Conferences on New Methods in Language Processing and Computational Natural Language Learning, NeMLaP3/CoNLL '98*, 151–160. 10.3115/1603899.1603924

Sauper & Barzilay. (2009). *Automatically generating wikipedia articles: A structure-aware approach*. Academic Press.

Sugiyama, K., & Kan, M. (2010). Scholarly paper recommendation via user's recent research interests. *Proceedings of the 2010 Joint International Conference on Digital Libraries, JCDL 2010*, 29–38. 10.1145/1816123.1816129

Sun, Y., Barber, R., Gupta, M., Aggarwal, C., & Han, J. (2011). Co-author relationship prediction in heterogeneous bibliographic networks. *Advances in Social Networks Analysis and Mining (ASONAM), 2011 International Conference on*, 121–128. 10.1109/ASONAM.2011.112

Torres, R., McNee, S. M., Abel, M., Konstan, J. A., & Riedl, J. (2004). Enhancing digital libraries with techlens+. *Proceedings of the 4th ACM/IEEE-CS Joint Conference on Digital Libraries, JCDL '04*, 228–236.

Vellino, A. (2009). Recommending journal articles with pagerank ratings. *Recommender Systems 2009*.

Voorhees, E. (1998). Variations in relevance judgments and the measurement of retrieval effectiveness. In *Information Processing and Management* (pp. 315–323). ACM Press.

Voorhees, E. M. (2000). Variations in relevance judgments and the measurement of retrieval effectiveness. *Information Processing & Management, 36*(5), 697–716. doi:10.1016/S0306-4573(00)00010-8

Ye, Chua, Kan, & Qiu. (2007). Document concept lattice for text understanding and summarization. *Information Processing & Management, 43*(6), 1643 – 1662. doi:10.1016/j.ipm.2007.03.010

ENDNOTES

[1]   This is one of the drawbacks of this system.

[2]   That was expected to be a disadvantage since the system rely on the citation score.

3   For evaluating a recommender, we consider the first 30 papers that a system returns and will use these returned papers as an input for evaluation in section 5.

4   https://dblp.uni-trier.de/

5   Using the institutional rights.

6   https://acl-arc.comp.nus.edu.sg/

7   These are similarities based on the documents title, abstract, title-abstract and full-text.

Chapter 7

Content–Determined Web Page Segmentation and Navigation for Mobile Web Searching

ABSTRACT

Nowadays the usage of mobile phones is widely spread in our lifestyle; we use cell phones as a camera, a radio, a music player, and even as a web browser. Since most web pages are created for desktop computers, navigating through web pages is highly fatigued. Hence, there is a great interest in computer science to adopt such pages with rich content into small screens of our mobile devices. On the other hand, every web page has got many different parts that do not have the equal importance to the end user. Consequently, the authors propose a mechanism to identify the most useful part of a web page to a user regarding his or her search query while the information loss is avoided. The challenge here comes from the fact that long web contents cannot be easily displayed in both vertical and horizontal ways.

INTRODUCTION

Web searching on a mobile device, especially based on a cell phone is very common and convenient. Since most Web pages are with rich content and mainly are specifically developed for desktop computers, it is hard to navigate them with (relatively) small screen of handled devices. Hence, there is a great interest in computer science to adopt such pages with rich content into small

DOI: 10.4018/978-1-7998-0961-6.ch007

screens of mobile devices. However, a Web page has different parts that do not have equal importance to the end user. This fact made us to consider a novel approach to identify the most useful portion of a Web page to the end user regarding its search query. Typically, mobile phones are common in the following characteristics:

- **Small Screen**: limited screen area compared to a conventional PC.
- **Limited Keyboard**: Limited area for interaction with the device. Therefore it is necessary to put the relevant part at first.
- **Distracted User:** A desktop user is mainly in an (relatively) isolated environment with focused attention to its working. Whereas, a smartphone user may be in an open area with distractive surrounding which makes him or her to devote only a portion of his or her attention to the device. Consequently, less scrolling is desired.

MOTIVATION

At (Kamvar et al., 2009) a log-based research for 3 different types of devices has been conducted based on, a common Smartphone[1], desktop computers and conventional phones; to see the behavior of users in regards to different devices in Web searching. The authors of the paper claimed that in their first order analysis of web search across computers, Smartphone, and conventional mobile phones, they have consistently found that search patterns on a Smartphone relatively mimics search patterns on computers. On the other hand, mobile search behavior is distinctly different. The authors claimed this might be due to advanced entry of a Smartphone compared to that on a mobile phone. Thus they predicted that as mobile devices become more advanced, users will treat mobile search as an extension of computer-based search. Hence the authors of this article concluded this might be caused due to the fact that a mobile phone has a small screen and the text-entry device is difficult to use- so users preferred to use mobile phones just once for performing a search. Theses distinct users' behaviors between Smartphone users and conventional cell phone users come from the smaller screen and button-based keyboards vs. touch screen of Smartphone.

While this study was conducted in the past and Smartphone users are the majority, the content of Web sites/portals has significantly changed and became much richer compared to the past. Consequently, there would be still needs of taking into account a mechanism which serves handled device users in Web searching in a way that the effort for reaching to the main content is minimized,

RELATED WORK

Content-Distance Model

Authors in (Sugaya, 2007) have proposed the architecture of a page segmentation based on content-distance. The approach is basically based on checking a page score and the distance of the content according to the distance in the source code of the corresponding Web page. Issues with this approach can be categorized as followings:

- The distance between elements in the code and between corresponding elements in the actual page might be different, i.e., the distance between 2 cells in the source code vs. the distance of corresponding cells in the actual table in the actual Web page.
- Most Web pages contain numerous parts which makes the introduced method slow and time-intensive.
- The low accuracy of the proposed method (55-70% based on the authors report) makes it not a desirable technique.

The proposed solution (a hybrid version of the framework) still can be time-intensive for the fact it needs to check a considerable sets of conditions.

Efforts on displaying web pages on small screens fall into following categories:

Transformation of a Web Page Layout for Small Displays

To assist users' with small screen during Web searching, Opera (Opera Software ASA, n.d.) suggested to transfer the lay out to a vertical long version. Chen et al. (Chen et al., 2003a) and Masuda et al. (Masuda et al., 2004) suggested displaying each column of a table side by side to the column's name.

A menu-like approach is proposed by Buchanan and Jones et al. (Buchanan et al., 2001), (Jones et al., 2002) which uses the site map of a Web page. A

Web design approach called Responsive Web design (RWD) is presented. The aim of this model is to engage developers to specifically design a version of Web page for mobile users (Marcotte, 2010).

Segmentation of a Web Page

DOM-Based Web Page Segmentation

A DOM-based segmentation is proposed by Kuppusamy and Aghila (Kuppusamy & Aghila, 2012), (Kuppusamy & Aghila, 2014) which groups a Web page content into two types of blocks based on appearance of child nodes in these blocks, they are called block-level and non block-level nodes. By analyzing the text density of each node regarding a threshold, the node content would be either represented as an individual segment or merged with nearest block-level node.

Liu et al. (Liu et al., 2011) proposed a page segmentation algorithm based on the Gomory-Hu tree in a planar graph. The edges and vertices show the leaf nodes and their relationship to each other. After building this graph, the Gomory-Hu is applied to the graph for the purpose of Web page segmentation. Kalaivani and Rajkumar (Kalaivani & Rajkumar, 2012a)[15] and Kang et al. (Kang et al., 2010) introduced a new method of Web page segmentation which takes into account the repetitive patterns of tags in a DOM tree structure of a Web page.

Page Segmentation Based on Page Layouts

Dividing a Web page into smaller segments based on content distance and layout information is proposed by Hattori et al. (Hattori et al., 2007). The concept of content distance is based on the distance of elements in the HTML code of a Web page. Song et al. (Song et al., 2004) adopted a block importance model for web page segmentation. The authors of this research employed vision-based page segmentation (VIPS) algorithm to partition a web page into a hierarchy semantic blocks.

By combining xhtml layout of a Web page with VIPS algorithm, Wu et al. (Wu et al., 2011) introduced a new algorithm called BGBPS (Block Gathering Based Page Segmentation). The main procedure of this algorithm is based on adoption of some tags such as < div > and < table > for archiving the page layout. A comparison of DOM-based segmentation and VIPS algorithms is given in Akpnar and Yesilada (Akpinar & Yesilada, 2013). The author then concluded that applying both techniques would give more convenient Web page segmentation.

Similarly, Sanoja and Ganc arsk (Sanoja & Gancarsk, 2013)[23](Sanoja & Ganarsk, 2014) proposed a hybrid segmentation model that takes advantage of VIPS and geometric models and called it Block-o-Matic, The focus of this model is to take into account the spatial property of a Web page and neglecting the textual attribute.. Four rules are applied to recognize different blocks in each page, taking the inline and line-break elements of HTML pages in account.

Semantic Page Segmentation

Contents: Chen et al. (Chen et al., 2005)[26] used high-level content information such as footers and headears to identify Web page separators and thus, segment corresponding Web page accordingly. Xie et al. (Xie et al., 2005) employed the block importance model to assign importance values to different segments of a web page, and displayed the result pages from the highest priority to the least.-

Adoption of machine learning techniques for Web page segmentation based on entropy reduction and decision tree is what Baluja (Baluja, 2006) introduced in his research work. A page splitting technique is proposed (Fraying & Sommerer, 2002) which clusters elements of a page into cohesive hroups and allows users to zoom in to each cluster. Using Rapid Serial Visual Presentation (RSVP), De Bruijn et al. (Bruijn et al., 2002) implemented a Web browsing tool. By incorporating usage of Wireless Markup Language (WML) cards, they deployed Web page segmentation by switching between different cards.

The CMo system, developed by Borodin et al. (Borodin et al., 2007a) (Mahmud et al., 2007)[35], partitions a Web page on following a link by a user. It uses some topic-boundary detection tools and fragments a Web pge. Doing so, it allows users to see and navigate between these portions of a Web page.

Web Page Summarization and Key Phrases Extraction for Thumbnail View

Web page segmentation based on summarizing the content is introduced in (Leoncini et al., 2012). By extracting textual content and applying common pre-processing methods such as stop-word removal and semantic networks, the framework breaks the textual content of a Web page into different concepts. By clustering each relevant concept into cohesive groups, the framework would assist users with relevant portion of a particular Web page regarding the selected topic.

Yang and Wang (Yang & Wang, 2003) presented a fractal theory based mathematical way for summarizing a Web page into a tree structure. The tree structure is based on WML cards and users, similarly to (Bruijn et al., 2002), can navigate within different cards. The most relevant sentences would be enlarged to attract users' interests. Fractal views are utilized to filter the less important nodes in the document structure. Buyukkokten et al. (Buyukkokten et al., 2001a)[39](Buyukkokten et al., 2000) represented a Web page summary by representing it with important keywords and sentences. The user can then dig in into the content of the page to discover relevant parts of the page.

A thumbnail view of a Web page for summarizing a Web page is introduced in (Bj¨ork et al., 1999). In a similar vein, Lam and Baudisch (Lam & Baudisch, 2005) also proposed a summary thumbnail view of a page, making the text fragments of thumbnail view of a page readable. Jones et al. (Jones et al., 2004) implemented a key-based view of a Web page for small screen devices. Each keyphrase is extracted from the textual content of the corresponding Web page. By clicking on a particular keyphrase, the user is able to view a Web page in either key-level or sentence level representations.

Important Regions Identification and Noise Removal

Yin and Lee (Yin & Lee, 2004) transferred a Web page into a graph and gave weight to each node of the graph according to a link analysis method, similar to one of Google PageRank on the basis of elements of an HTML DOM tree. Noise elimination from a Web page was also studied.. Htwe and Kham (Htwe & Kham, 2011) used DOM and neural networks together for data extraction by removing noises from a certain page. To do so, they built a DOM tree and by training a data set using neural network, a threshold is examined to the tree and the rest of the tree with deeper depth will be removed as they are regarded as noise.

AUTOMATIC PAGE SCROLLING BASED ON DOM TREE

In this article, our effort is to incorporate use of DOM[2] tree (data object model) for Web page segmentation and accordingly, presenting the most relevant segment to the user by an auto-focus mechanism. A DOM tree is a W3C standard for letting programming codes to access and manipulate the content and structure of a (Web) document. The structure of this platform is based on a tree which its nodes represents objects of a Web page. The DOM tree is language independent and works with XML and HTML documents.

To use DOM tree for our purpose, we should first answer this question: "how to use DOM tree to apply Web page scrolling?" Using DOM tree, we can try to Web page Segmentation by considering leaf nodes of same parent node as a segment of a page. On the other word, those sibling nodes which yield no more can be taken into account as a segment of a page.

In the followings, we brought details of steps for the process of automatic Web page scrolling based on DOM tree,

Main Procedure

In order to assist mobile Web searching with an auto-focus gadget, we implemented the framework in a client-server structure. At the client side, we launch a browser engine to collect a user's keyword and the URL address of a Web page that the user clicks on it. On the other hand, on the server side, we will do some appropriate computation in order to do the page segmentation and accordingly, spot the most relevant segment of the page in respect to the user's search query.

The overall steps for this matter can be summarized as followings:

1.   Extracting user's search query and URL string of clicked Web page.
2.   Performing a post-order traverse through the DOM tree of corresponding Web page and getting the raw text.
3.   Using leaf nodes to segment the Web page.
4.   Apply Stop word removal for raw text of each segment
5.   Apply stemming

6. Calculate term frequency-inverse document frequency (tf-idf) values for each stemmed word.
7. Calculate posterior probability for each stemmed keyword of each segment.
8. Apply 4-7 for user's keywords.
9. Choose the segment with the closest posterior value to the one for user's keywords

Data Extraction

First step for implementing the proposed approach is to gain the required data from user's input. To make this step dependent from client specifications, we chose following two public source of information:

1. URL address of the browser (for SERP)
2. Browser changes of its status.

URL Address

By performing a Web searching task, a commercial search engine would generate a result page, aka SERP. By considering hidden data within URL-strings of each result page, we can extract useful information. These URLs follow a common pattern although slightly differs from a search engines to another. For example, if we perform 3 different search queries in Google and Yahoo!, we might get following URLs:

1. tsunami
   a. Google: http://www.google.com.hk/search?hl=zh-CN&source=hp&q=tsunamii&gbv=2
   b. Yahoo!: http://search.yahoo.com/search;_ylt=AspxmAIYhiLR3izolt3fhESbvZx4?p=tsunami&toggle=1&cop=mss&ei=UTF-8&fr=yfp-t-521
2. flood
   a. Google: http://www.google.com.hk/search?hl=zh-CN&source=hp&q=flood&gbv=2
   b. Yahoo!: http://search.yahoo.com/search;_ylt=AspxmAIYhiLR3izolt3fhESbvZx4?p=flood&toggle=1&cop=mss&ei=UTF-8&fr=yfp-t-521
3. camping

a.   Google: http://www.google.com.hk/
     search?hl=zh-CN&source=hp&q=camping&gbv=2
b.   Yahoo!: http://search.yahoo.com/search;_ylt=AspxmAIYhiL
     R3izolt3fhESbvZx4?p=camping&toggle=1&cop=mss&ei=U
     TF-8&fr=yfp-t-521

If we take a closer look at Google results, we can notice that a similar pattern is being applied before and after the keywords in the URL. There is a part repeated in all 3 examples from *http* until right before *q* (which probably stands for query):

"http://www.google.com.hk/search?hl=zh-CN&source=hp&q="

Right after this part, user's query is occurred. Similar behavior is spotted with Yahoo. Using regular expressions, we can extract the useful data out of a particular expression. In the context of this research, we can introduce following regex (short for regular expression) for Google and Yahoo:

1.   For Google
     a.   http://www\\.google\\.com\\.hk/search\\?hl\\=zh-CN\\&source\\=
          hp\\&q=([^&]+).*";
2.   For Yahoo!
     a.   http://search\\.yahoo\\.com\\/search\\;_ylt\\= AspxmAIYhiLR3iz
          olt3fhESbvZx4//&p=([^&]+).*";

The keyword will be extracted by ([^&]+) operator . The () operator tells the regex to extract whatever that matches the pattern surrounded by it. In order to be able to find the most appropriate segment of a Web page based on a user's query, we need to acquire the corresponding query by applying this regex to the URL address of the corresponding SERP.

Traversing a DOM Tree

In order to be able to gather raw data for segmenting a Web page we need to collect the raw textual data from HTML source code of corresponding Web page. To do as such, we transferred HTML source code of a Web page into a DOM tree. Our strategy for segmentation, as we mentioned earlier, is based on the leaf nodes of a parent node. Considering these nodes which are referred to as siblings, we can segment a Web page into logical segments.

We take into account these segments as a document for the computation of TF-IDF values. (See next section)

To achieve higher performance, we decided to apply stop word filtering, that is, to remove frequent common keywords such as "a", "the", "is" from the raw data. Another common step for text mining is to apply "Stemming". The idea behind stemming is to reduce a word to its root word or "stem".

For stop word removal, we used a common set of English stop words. In each iteration over a node value, we apply this list to the raw text extracted from the corresponding node value.

After acquiring a "bag of words", then we proceed to produce stemmed words. There are different algorithms to apply for stemming. The one that being chosen here is suffix-stripping. Suffix stripping algorithms do not rely on a lookup table. Instead, there are a set of rules to produce the root words such as followings:

- if the word ends in 'ed', remove the 'ed'.
- if the word ends in 'ing', remove the 'ing'.
- if the word ends in 'ly', remove the 'ly'.

Measuring Term Frequency-Inverse Document Frequency

Toward for adopting the classifier to the architecture, we need a set of training data, categories that we need to classify the data into and features for the classifier for grouping the training data. So, in this method, the training data are stemmed words, the categories are the segments of the page and the feature for grouping is the tf-idf value of the words. So it seems that these values are so important. To calculate the tf (term frequency) simply first count the whole word of each segment and then count the number of occurrence of the stemmed word in the corresponding segment, Then dividing second value by first value:

$$tf[i] = \frac{wordCount[i]}{N}$$

Where the $tf[i]$ is tf value for i[th] stemmed word, word Count[i] is equal to the number of occurrence for the ith word and the N is equal to the total number of the stemmed word. The next step is to calculate the value of idf(inverse document frequency). To do this, we need to identify two variables: the number of documents (which we adopted it as number of the segments of the page) and the number of the times that the corresponding stemmed is happened. If remember, while we were discussing about traversing through the DOM, I mentioned the way to calculate the number of segments, so now, we have the value of the first value. For getting the second's, we should use *Matchers* to detect the stemmed words that having the same pattern.

$$idf\left[i\right] = \log \frac{seg}{approvedSegs\left[i\right]}$$

where *idf*[*i*] is equal to the idf for the ith stemmed word and seg is equal to the number of segments of the page and ApprovedSegs[i] is equal to the number of the segments that i^{th} stemmed words appears within them. Finally, by multiplying *idf*[*i*] by *tf*[*i*], we can compute value of *TFIDF* for the ith stemmed keyword as in followings:

TFIDF[*i*] = *tf*[*i*] * *idf*[*i*]

To calculate ApprovedSegs[i] we need a mechanism for detecting the stemmed words and its position. We managed to take advantage of Xpath principle. The usage of Xpath in this work, includes identification of a word's occurrence within a specific DOM node. In this article we have used Xpath to locate the position of occurrence of a word . Corresponding Xpath expression that is applied in the context of this book is as follow:

String expression = "//*[contains(translate(text( ),
'ABCDEFGHIJKLMNOPQRSTUVWXYZ',
'abcdefghijklmnopqrstuvwxyz'), $term)]";

Adopting Classifier

In previous steps, we prepared for applying the classifier to my program. To do this, we needed to get a weight for our classifier. In this case, we choose the tf-idf value. Now that we have the all words tf-idf values, we can apply the classifier. But before doing this, we need to get the mean and variance of this values. Abstractly, the probability model for a classifier is a conditional model:

$P(C| F_1, ..., F_n)$

Where C is a dependent variable and F_1 to F_n are predators/features. Using Bayes' theorem, we can write:

$$P\left(C \mid F_1, \ldots, F_n\right) = \frac{P(C)\left(F_1, \ldots, F_n\right)}{P\left(F_1, \ldots, F_n\right)}$$

In plain English the above equation can be written as:

$$Posterior = \frac{prior * likelihood}{evidence}$$

What we need now is to adopt this to our work. Posterior probability here would be the probability of ith segment of a Web page to be selected for auto scrolling in respect to a user's searching query to be occurred within it. Prior probability, $P(i^{th}segment)$, would be the probability of a segment of a page to be selected regardless of any conditions. This is basically equal to $\frac{m}{n}$ here m is the number of root words within content of ith segment an n is the total number of root words within the content of the corresponding Web page. Likelihood can be formulated as below:

Liklihood $= P(Query| i^{th}segment$.

In other words, it is equal to probability of a search query to be occurred in i^{th} segment of a Web page. This would be computed by dividing number of occurrences of Query to the total number of root words in i^{th} segment. Last but not least, evidence is equal to $P(Query)$ which is equal for all cases and thus can be removed from the computation.

To calculate likelihood, we can consider the normal distribution of the part as follows:

$$P\left(Query \mid i^{th}\ segment\right) = \frac{1}{\sqrt{2\pi\sigma^2}} \exp^{\frac{-\left(Query_{TF-IDF} - \mu\right)^2}{2o^2}}$$

Where μ and $\sigma2$ are mean and variance of the corresponding query.

Auto-Focus

The proposed framework will start working once a user performs a searching query and choosing a Web page to be loaded. The framework is based on local client server architecture. The client part is where the user is assisted with a copy of a browser and the server part is where we perform computation for refining the most relevant segment of a Web page regarding a user's query.

At this point, the structure would call the browser engine[3] to grab the status change regarding the action of user's tapping. The browser engine would pass several different URLs between client and server[4] as a part of three-way handshake. Once we detect URL of the corresponding URL and the user's keyword, we would store them for further analysis.

First step is to build a DOM tree from the source code of Web page and afterwards, performing a posterior traverse through it for the sake of Web page segmentation. Next step is a lexical analysis. We would apply stop-word filtering to the textual content of the Web page in order to clean the raw data. Furthermore, stemming would be performed to gather more terms under same word family.

Now we can compute TF-IDF value for each root node by performing another traversing through DOM node. By knowing values of TF-IDF, we can compute normal distribution for each user's keyword. At the same time, we use Xpath to store the position (as in which segment of the page) of each user's keyword. Later on we can use this information for applying auto-focus to the appropriate segment of the Web page.

EVALUATION

Setting

The server used in this evaluation has a server with CPU of 1.83 GHz and RAM of 1 GB, examining 4 keywords upon web search engine and calculating the time that the algorithm spends to find the proper portion of the page for laying out and also the accuracy of the results. We categorized keywords in different groups. First group of keywords are singular keywords. Second group belongs to 2-term keywords (2 stemmed keywords) and last group is where users' keywords are plural. Table 1 shows an illustration of these categories

Table 1. The dataset being used in this evaluation

Singular keywords		Plural Keywords			
photography	longman	java book	study abroad	history of singapore	
Adventure rainbow	Art rainbow	how to pass an exam	most expensive city of the world	ways to gain confidence	
sport	Samsung	cooking pizza	how to fishing	green house effects	
Olympics	laptop	adventure racing	healthy diet	chocolate chip cookies	
Merlin	dress	pyramid of Giza	how to drive a car	do alien exist	
green	flood	Mount Kinabalu	angry birds	who is Sir Stamford Raffles	
hadoop	bags	when telephone invented?	public speaking	ways to fix shelf	
cartoons	sunset	what is origami	color codes	earn money	

Notation

Median

in statistics and probability theory, **median** is described as the numerical value separating the higher half of a sample, a population, or a probability distribution, from the lower half. The *median* of a finite list of numbers can be found by arranging all the observations from lowest value to highest value and picking the middle one. If there is an even number of observations, then there is no single middle value; the median is then usually defined to be the mean of the two middle values.

Mode

In statistics, the **mode** is the value that occurs most frequently in a data set or a probability distribution. In some fields, notably education, sample data are often called **scores**, and the sample mode is known as the **modal score**. Like the statistical mean and median, the mode is a way of capturing important information about a random variable or a population in a single quantity. The mode is in general different from the mean and median, and may be very different for strongly skewed distributions.

Standard Deviation (Std Deviation)

In statistics and probability theory, **standard deviation** (represented by the symbol σ) shows how much variation or "dispersion" exists from the average (mean, or expected value). A low standard deviation indicates that the data points tend to be very close to the mean, whereas high standard deviation indicates that the data points are spread out over a large range of values.

Stem and Leaf Plot

Data can be shown in a variety of ways including graphs, charts and tables. A Stem and Leaf Plot is a type of graph that is similar to a histogram but shows more information. The Stem-and-Leaf Plot summarizes the shape of a set of data (the distribution) and provides extra detail regarding individual values. The data is arranged by place value. The digits in the largest place are referred to as the stem and the digits in the smallest place are referred to as the leaf (leaves). The leaves are displayed to the right of the stem. Stem and Leaf Plots are great organizers for large amounts of information.

Result

The overall results of Singular keywords are shown in Table 2. Here we can say, based on the time, usually it takes 4.5 sec to find the results for single keywords. This shows also that because the Std deviation is low, so most of the values are around the average time.

The results for first group of plural keywords (keywords with two terms, excluding stop words) are shown in Table 3. For this group; we can see that the mean and median are higher than last group. It may concluded as that increasing the number of keywords from one to two, made to open the result longer with average of 0.67 sec. but based on lower standard deviation it shows the time for this group is closer to the mean compared to the other group.

Results of second group of plural keywords (keywords with more than two terms) are shown in Table 4. The accuracy got even lower by nearly 10% though the time consumed to find the relevant information did not change much.

Table 2. Results over singular keywords

Keyword	Time (sec)	URL
adventure	4.1	www.adventure.com/
photography	4.2	https://www.photography.com/
sport	9.3	www.discoverhongkong.com/eng/events/sports.html
Olympics	5.7	https://www.hotelolympic.com/
Merlin	10.9	https://www.sentosa.com.sg/en/attractions/imbiah-lookout/the-merlion/
green	3.1	https://www.enb.gov.hk/en/Green_HK/index.html
hadoop	3.2	http://hadoop.apache.org/
cartoons	3.3	https://www.glasbergen.com/
Sabah	3.2	http://www.sabahtourism.com/
rainbow	5.1	https://rainbowsystem.com/
longman	3.1	https://www.ldoceonline.com/
Samsung	2.9	http://drive.seagate.com/content/samsung-en-us
laptop	3.1	http://www.eboxgz.com/
dress	3.2	www.simplydresses.com
flood	2.2	https://www.fema.gov/hazard/flood/index.shtm
bags	4.8	http://www.thebaglady.tv/
sunset	3.9	https://sunrisesunset.willyweather.com.au/
beach	3.7	https://en.wikipedia.org/wiki/Beaches_of_Hong_Kong
art	4.7	https://www.hongkongartfair.com/

CONCLUSION

In this chapter, we demonstrated a DOM-based architecture to display Web pages for small screen devices. Unlike previous attempts on changing the layout of Web page either by transforming its structure of breaking it into summarized regions, our proposal keeps the original structure sacrosanct by auto-scrolling the focus of Web browser to the most relevant part of the Web page regarding a user's keyword.

Table 3. Results over first plural group of keywords

Keyword	Time (sec)	URL
java book	4.2	http://www.techbooksforfree.com/java.shtml
cooking pizza	4.8	http://step-by-step-cook.co.uk/mains/pizza/
adventure racing	4.2	http://www.arworldseries.com/
pyramid of Giza	3.1	www.sevenwondersworld.com/wonders_of_world_giza_pyramid.html
Mount Kinabalu	5	http://www.climbmtkinabalu.com
when telephone invented?	3	http://inventors.about.com/od/bstartinventors/a/telephone.htm
what is origami	4	http://library.thinkquest.org/5402/history.html
successful study	4.8	http://www.adprima.com/studyout.htm
earn money	6.6	http://www.freebyte.com/makemoney/
study abroad	3.1	https://www.vistawide.com/studyabroad/why_study_abroad.htm
how to fishing	2.9	https://www.takemefishing.org/fishing/fishopedia/how-to-fish
healthy diet	8	http://www.wellnessletter.com/ucberkeley/foundations/13-keys-to-a-healthy-diet/
how to drive a car	7	https://www.wikihow.com/Drive-a-Car-With-an-Automatic-Transmission
angry birds	4.9	http://www.angrybirdsriogame.com/
public speaking	6.1	http://www.stresscure.com/jobstress/speak.html
color codes	6.8	https://www.computerhope.com/htmcolor.htm
HTML codes	5	http://www.htmlcodetutorial.com/
china Airlines	9.1	https://www.airlinequality.com/Forum/china.htm

Table 4. Results over second plural group of keywords

Keyword	Time (sec)	URL
history of singapore	5.9	http://www.newasia-singapore.com/travel_information/introduction/brief_history_of_singapore_200705304.html
green house effects	3	https://www.ucar.edu/learn/1_3_1.htm
chocolate chip cookies	8.1	https://www.joyofbaking.com/ChocolateChipCookies.html
do alien exist	6	http://www.msnbc.msn.com/id/28148553/ns/technology_and_science-space/t/six-frontiers-alien-life/#.QtS_HVJtiPE
who is Sir Stamford Raffles	5.9	http://www.britannica.com/EBchecked/topic/489451/Sir-Stamford-Raffles
ways to fix shelf	4.5	https://www.ehow.co.uk/how_6609528_fix-floating-shelf.html
how to pass an exam	5.8	https://www.explainthatstuff.com/howtopassexams.html
ways to gain confidence	6.1	http://www.essortment.com/gain-confidence-life-54988.html
most expensive city of the world	10.3	https://en.wikipedia.org/wiki/List_of_most_expensive_cities_for_expatria

REFERENCES

Akpinar, M. E., & Yesilada, Y. (2013). Vision based page segmentation algorithm: Extended and perceived success. *Current Trends in Web Engineering - ICWE 2013 International Workshops ComposableWeb, QWE, MDWE, DMSSW, EMotions, CSE, SSN, and PhD Symposium. Revised Selected Papers*, 238–252. 10.1007/978-3-319-04244-2_22

Baluja, S. (2006). Browsing on small screens: Recasting web-page segmentation into an efficient machine learning framework. *Proc. of WWW*, 33–42. 10.1145/1135777.1135788

Bj¨ork, S., Holmquist, L., Redstr¨om, J., Bretan, I., Danielsson, R., & Karlgren, J. (1999). WEST: A web browser for small terminals. *Proc. of UIST*, 187–196. 10.1145/320719.322601

Borodin, Mahmud, & Ramakrishnan. (2007a). Context browsing with mobiles - when less is more. *Proc. of MobiSys*, 3–5.

Borodin, Y., Mahmud, J., & Ramakrishnan, I. (2007b). CSurf: A context-driven non-visual web-browser. *Proc. of WWW*, 31–40.

Bruijn, O. D., Spence, R., & Chong, M. (2002, September). RSVP browser: Web browsing on small screen devices. *Personal and Ubiquitous Computing*, 6(4), 245–252. doi:10.1007007790200024

Buchanan, G., Farrant, S., Jones, M., & Thimbleby, H. (2001). Improving mobile internet usability. *Proc. of WWW*. 10.1145/371920.372181

Buyukkokten, O. (2002). Efficient Web Browsing on Handheld Devices Using Page and Form Summa- rization. *ACM Transactions on Information Systems*, 20(1), 82–115. doi:10.1145/503104.503109

Buyukkokten, O., Garcia-Molina, H., & Paepcke, A. (2001a). Accordion summarization for end-game browsing on pdas and cellular phones. *Proc. of CHI*, 213–220. 10.1145/365024.365102

Buyukkokten, O., Garcia-Molina, H., & Paepcke, A. (2001b). Seeing the whole in parts: Text summarization for web browsing on handheld devices. *Proc. of WWW*, 652–662. 10.1145/371920.372178

Buyukkokten, O., Garcia-Molina, H., Paepcke, A., & Winograd, T. (2000). Power browser: Efficient web browsing for pdas. *Proc. of CHI*, 430–437. 10.1145/332040.332470

Chen, Y., Ma, W., & Zhang, H. (2003a). Improving web browsing on small devices based on table classification. *Proc. of WWW.*

Chen, Y., Ma, W., & Zhang, H. (2003b). Detecting web page structure for adaptive viewing on small form factor. *Proc. of WWW,* 225–233. 10.1145/775152.775184

Chen, Y., Xie, X., Ma, W., & Zhang, H. (2005). Adapting web pages for small screen devices. *IEEE Internet Computing, 9*(1), 50–56. doi:10.1109/MIC.2005.5

Fraying, N., & Sommerer, R. (2002). Smartview: Flexible viewing of web page contents. *Proc. of WWW.*

Hattori, G., Hoashi, K., Matsumoto, K., & Sugaya, F. (2007). Robust web page segmentation for mobile terminal using content-distances and page layout information. *Proc. of WWW,* 361–370. 10.1145/1242572.1242622

Htwe & Kham. (2011). Extracting data region in web page by removing noise using DOM and neural network. *Proc. of Information and Financial Engineering,* 123–128.

Jones, M., Buchanan, G., & Thimbleby, H. (2002). Sorting out searching on small screen devices. *Proc. of HCI.* 10.1007/3-540-45756-9_8

Jones, S., Jones, M., & Deo, S. (2004, February). Using keyphrases as search result surrogates on small screen devices. *Personal and Ubiquitous Computing, 8*(1).

Kalaivani, & Rajkumar. (2012a). Reappearance layout based web page segmentation for small screen devices. *International Journal of Computers and Applications, 49*(20).

Kalaivani & Rajkumar. (2012b). Dynamic web page segmentation based on detecting reappearance and layout of tag patterns for small screen devices. *IEEE Conference Proceedings,* 508–513.

Kamvar, M., Kellar, M., & Patel, R. (2009). Computers and iPhones and Mobile Phones, oh my! WWW international conference, 801-810.

Kang, J., Yang, J., & Choi, J. (2010). Repetition-based web page segmentation by detecting tag patterns for small-screen devices. *IEEE Transactions on Consumer Electronics, 56*(2), 980–986. doi:10.1109/TCE.2010.5506029

Kuppusamy & Aghila. (2014). Caseper: An efficient model for personalized web page change detection based on segmentation. *Journal of King Saud University-Computer and Information Sciences, 26*(1), 19–27.

Kuppusamy, K., & Aghila, G. (2012, January). A personalized web page content filtering model based on segmentation. *International Journal of Information Sciences and Techniques, 2*(1), 41–51. doi:10.5121/ijist.2012.2104

Lam, & Baudisch. (2005). Summary thumbnails: Readable overviews for small screen web browsers. *Proc. of CHI*, 689–690.

Leoncini, A., Sangiacomo, F., Gastaldo, P., & Zunino, R. (2012). *A semantic based framework for summarization and page segmentation in web mining.* InTech. doi:10.5772/51178

Liu, X., Lin, H., & Tian, Y. (2011, December). Segmenting webpage with gomory-hu tree based clustering. *Journal of Software, 6*(12), 2421–2425. doi:10.4304/jsw.6.12.2421-2425

Mahmud, Borodin, Ramakrishnan, & Das. (2007). *Combating information overload in non-visual web access using context.* Academic Press.

Marcotte. (2010, May). Responsive web design. *A List Apart.*

Masuda, H., Tsukamoto, S., Yasutomi, S., & Nakagawa, H. (2004). Recognition of HTML table structure. *Proc. of IJCNLP.*

Opera Software ASA. (n.d.). *Small screen rendering.* http://www.opera.com/ products/ obile/smallscreen/

Sanoja & Gancarsk. (2013). Block-o-matic: a web page segmentation tool and its evaluation. *BDA2013, 1*, 1–5.

Sanoja, A., & Ganarsk, S. (2012). Yet another hybrid segmentation tool. *Proceedings of the 9th International Conference on Preservation of Digital Objects.*

Sanoja, A., & Ganarsk, S. (2014). Block-o-matic: A web page segmentation framework. *International Conference on Multimedia Computing and Systems*, 595–600.

Song, R., Liu, H., Wen, J., & Ma, W. (2004). Learning block importance models for web pages. *Proc. of WWW*, 203–211. 10.1145/988672.988700

Sugaya, F. (2007). *Robust Web Page Segmentation for Mobile Terminal Using Content-Distances and Page Layout Information.* ACM.

Wu, L., He, N. Y., & Ke, Y. (2011). A block gathering based on mobile webpage segmentation algorithm. *Proceedings of IEEE 10th International Conference on Trust, Security and Privacy in Computing and Communications*, 1425–1430.

Xie, X., Miao, G., Song, R., Wen, J., & Ma, W. (2005). Efficient browsing of web search results on mobile devices based on block importance model. *Proc. of PERCOM*, 17–26.

Yang, C., & Wang, F. (2003). Fractal summarization for mobile devices to access large documents on the web. *Proc. of WWW*, 215–224. 10.1145/775152.775183

Yin, X., & Lee, W. (2004). Using link analysis to improve layout on mobile devices. *Proc. of WWW*. 10.1145/988672.988718

ENDNOTES

[1] Originally the authors made the study for iPhone. Since iPhone was a common Smartphone by then and for the sake of generalization, we replace it with this word.

[2] http://www.w3.org/DOM/

[3] We have used cobra browser engine for the purpose of this work.

[4] The actual client (our browser) and server (the server which hosts the corresponding Web page).

Conclusion

As internet has changed the way of living, Web searching has become an inevitable part of people's life. Nevertheless, since majority of internet users are novice, thus there are difficulties arisen while performing a Web search.

The aim of this book was to draw attentions to the importance of correct recommendation and visualization for Web search results. We illustrated the difficulties and discussed the shortcomings of the state-of-the-art for each particular case.

We have begun with defining the Web search result recommendation and visualization principle. Furthermore, we elaborated that currently, there are two main types of recommendation and visualization for such aim, namely, horizontal and vertical Web searching where the former refers to the general Web queries issued by users to get toa particular Web page, obtain a particular piece of information or service and the latter refers to more specified domain of Web searching. On the other hand, there are queries which target certain types of available documents on the Web such as PDFs and PPTs etc.

As a result, we selected three main concerns toward recommending and visualizing Web search results, i.e., Web search visualization for ambiguous queries, Web search recommendation for navigational searching and Web search recommendation for academic Web searching.

Consequently, this book has contributed in the following domains.

WEB SEARCH RECOMMENDATION

Web Search Recommendation for Navigational Queries

We showed that the state-of-the-art for Web search results recommendation for navigational searching is not according to its definition. Consequently, we proposed a recommendation methodology which takes the URL and the pattern of query occurrence within the URL-string into account. By defining navigational and non-navigational resources, thereby we are able to build a concept lattice of URLs. Applying formal concept analysis over this lattice as a method for producing a candidate set of URLs, thus we are able to pull out those URLs that are more propel to be the required navigational resource.

To rank these candidate URLs, we introduced a weighting algorithm called lattice_lift which gives different weights to URLs based on their format and the pattern of occurrence of a user's navigational query within that URL-string.

Based on the evaluation results, we showed that first of all, using introduced strategy would give a higher chance of users' first clicks on the navigational resources. Moreover, we illustrated the fact that there is a correlation between clicking on navigational resources and the mutual information between the navigational resource and the size of candidate sets. In other words, the smaller the size of a candidate set the higher chance of a user's first click on a navigational resource. In addition, we demonstrates the fact that our proposed model ranks navigational resources in higher positions with less noises compared to the state-of-the-art

Web Search Recommendation for Scholarly Documents

We studied the shortcomings of current vertical search engines and current in-use techniques for recommendation toward Web search results for scholarly documents. By considering issues such as Matthew effect, privacy issue and time-intensive nature of state-of-the-art for recommending scientific articles according to an input query, we are motivated to develop a recommender to overcome this dilemma.

In order to remove current fatigues in scholarly recommendation, we came up with a summary-based recommender that uses summaries of papers to omit the time-intensive nature of full-text methods. Moreover, it vanishes the privacy issue, problem of Matthew effect and other existing shortcoming of current recommenders.

According to the results of the evaluation, Bathan outperforms baselines based on mean F1-measure while Google scholar resulted into better precisions.

On the basis of skewness, Bathan gives less spread out results compared to baselines for both ranking policies. That means relevant documents listed by Bathan have much closer relation to each other from top to bottom. In addition, Bathan has a better mutual information using Levenshtein edit distance to rank relevant documents compared to the time when we used Cosine similarity.

In the meantime, this study showed that first of all, different content-determined judgments reacted differently for computing the similarity between different papers. That means each part of a paper carries a significantly different scent of a paper. Secondly, we showed that abstract of a paper does not comply as a comprehensive extractive summary of a paper.

Las but not least, Levenshtein edit distance improved the corresponding results produced similarity for all evaluation metrics.

As an improvement to Bathan, we introduced a mechanism to intellectually return similar papers based on one's publication record. To do as such, we proposed the principle of textual references to visual features which considers those fragments of textual content of a paper that has a reference to a visual feature such as a Figure or a Table. To prove the correctness of this assumption, we conducted three empirical studies to show how this principle distinguishes between similar and dissimilar papers of an author.

To show the effect of similarity of textual references to visual features on Bathan, we conducted an experiment in which we examined the evaluation's metrics on Bathan with and without this principle.

Our performance results based on the mean precision, recall, F_1 _measure and unanimous ranks shows that using the proposed improvement increases the precision and recall by 200% and F_1 _measure by 250% as well as it ranks relevant papers by more than 4 positions higher than the Bathan without the improvement.

Web Search Visualization

We argued the fact that there is not enough or even appropriate attention in regard to the visualization for an ambiguous query. Although there are few works which aimed involving visualization inWeb searching as a general aspect and for ambiguous searching in specific, however the inconsistency as well as vague nature of such techniques derived us to consider a more cohesive approach for such matter.

As a matter of fact, we introduced a visual and textual search snippet that consist of 4 different variations. The common elements of each variation are a relevantly extracted thumbnail from content of each Web page in respect to a user's ambiguous query together with a newly relevant textual search snippet. Our two users studies showed that using both relevant textual and visual elements of Web pages in order to assist users in disambiguation tasks provide users considerable assistance.

Web Usage Study

This has been shown that users' searching tasks can be categorized into 3 main groups, namely informational, navigational and transactional searching. Each of these categories is thereby elaborated into details. As a part of recommendation Web search results for navigational searching, we have conducted a Web log study to define categories for navigational resources.

Moreover, from the result of experiments for recommending relevant navigational resources to a user, since we have used two search logs from two different groups users with different language preferences, we noticed that Chinese users of Sogou reacted differently compared to the users of AOL. To dig this case further, we have conducted a comparative Web log study between AOL and SogouQ, two of search logs which are used in this book. Since both Web log transactions are collected at similar time periods, thus we believe any implication drawn from this study can be accurate and valid.

Based on the evaluations' results and the search usage study, we concluded following implications:

Considering the popularity of queries, we can say that based on issued queries, users from both search engines seem to be interested in comparatively similar topics, nonetheless the dramatic difference in the domain extensions of clicked-URLs of navigational resources, topical relevance of navigational queries of both search logs and session duration of navigational searching for either group of users, bring us into this conclusion that Chinese users and Sogou search engine have a significantly different habits of treatment toward navigational queries compared to AOL and its users.

Findings of this study can be used by commercial search engines and Webmasters to both improve the ranking and content of pages for navigational queries that are issued by non-native users.

Related Readings

To continue IGI Global's long-standing tradition of advancing innovation through emerging research, please find below a compiled list of recommended IGI Global book chapters and journal articles in the areas of navigational searching, resource identification, and ambiguous queries of Web searching These related readings will provide additional information and guidance to further enrich your knowledge and assist you with your own research.

Alharahsheh, H. H., & Pius, A. (2019). Creating Business Value and Competitive Advantage Through Glocalization. In V. Nadda, S. Bilan, M. Azam, & D. Mulindwa (Eds.), *Neoliberalism in the Tourism and Hospitality Sector* (pp. 83–98). IGI Global. doi:10.4018/978-1-5225-6983-1.ch005

Amer, A. A. (2019). Data Replication Impact on DDBS System Performance. In M. D. Lytras, N. Aljohani, E. Damiani, & K. Chui (Eds.), *Semantic Web Science and Real-World Applications* (pp. 134–162). IGI Global. doi:10.4018/978-1-5225-7186-5.ch006

Anbarasan, K., & Chitrakala, S. (2018). Clustering-Based Color Image Segmentation Using Local Maxima. *International Journal of Intelligent Information Technologies*, *14*(1), 28–47. doi:10.4018/IJIIT.2018010103

Andriopoulou, F., Birkos, K., & Lymberopoulos, D. (2017). A Novel Hierarchical Group-Based Overlay Healthcare Network. *International Journal of E-Health and Medical Communications*, *8*(4), 81–102. doi:10.4018/IJEHMC.2017100105

Arora, A., Srivastava, A., & Bansal, S. (2019). Graph and Neural Network-Based Intelligent Conversation System. In H. Banati, S. Mehta, & P. Kaur (Eds.), *Nature-Inspired Algorithms for Big Data Frameworks* (pp. 339–357). IGI Global. doi:10.4018/978-1-5225-5852-1.ch014

Backholm, K., Högväg, J., Lindholm, J., Knutsen, J., & Westvang, E. (2018). Promoting Situation Awareness. *International Journal of Information Systems for Crisis Response and Management*, *10*(1), 38–56. doi:10.4018/IJISCRAM.2018010103

Bagui, S., Mondal, A. K., & Bagui, S. (2019). Improving the Performance of kNN in the MapReduce Framework Using Locality Sensitive Hashing. *International Journal of Distributed Systems and Technologies*, *10*(4), 1–16. doi:10.4018/IJDST.2019100101

Barkhordari, M., & Niamanesh, M. (2017). Aras. *International Journal of Distributed Systems and Technologies*, *8*(2), 47–60. doi:10.4018/IJDST.2017040104

Barkhordari, M., & Niamanesh, M. (2018). Hengam a MapReduce-Based Distributed Data Warehouse for Big Data. *International Journal of Artificial Life Research*, *8*(1), 16–35. doi:10.4018/IJALR.2018010102

Barkhordari, M., Niamanesh, M., & Bakhshmandi, P. (2019). Baran. In M. Habib (Ed.), *Handbook of Research on the Evolution of IT and the Rise of E-Society* (pp. 124–161). IGI Global. doi:10.4018/978-1-5225-7214-5.ch007

Begum, B. S., & Ramasubramanian, N. (2019). Design of an Intelligent Data Cache with Replacement Policy. *International Journal of Embedded and Real-Time Communication Systems*, *10*(2), 87–107. doi:10.4018/IJERTCS.2019040106

Camacho, D. P., Pomar, J. M., & Hervás, J. C. (2019). Relationship Between Satisfaction and Social Perception of the Negative Impacts of Sporting Events. In M. A. Dos Santos (Ed.), *Integrated Marketing Communications, Strategies, and Tactical Operations in Sports Organizations* (pp. 147–171). IGI Global. doi:10.4018/978-1-5225-7617-4.ch008

Chantrapornchai, C., Kaegjing, A., Srakaew, S., Piyanuntcharatsr, W., & Krakhaeng, S. (2017). Utilizing Architecture Aspects for in Data Mining for Computer System Design. In S. Bhattacharyya, S. De, I. Pan, & P. Dutta (Eds.), *Intelligent Multidimensional Data Clustering and Analysis* (pp. 225–252). IGI Global. doi:10.4018/978-1-5225-1776-4.ch009

Chathalingath, A., & Manoharan, A. (2019). Performance Optimization of Tridiagonal Matrix Algorithm [TDMA] on Multicore Architectures. *International Journal of Grid and High Performance Computing, 11*(4), 1–12. doi:10.4018/IJGHPC.2019100101

Cherbal, S., Boukerram, A., & Boubetra, A. (2017). Locality-Awareness and Replication for an Adaptive CHORD to MANet. *International Journal of Distributed Systems and Technologies, 8*(3), 1–24. doi:10.4018/IJDST.2017070101

Collard, M., Collard, P., & Stattner, E. (2018). The Eternal-Return Model of Human Mobility and Its Impact on Information Flow. In N. Meghanathan (Ed.), *Graph Theoretic Approaches for Analyzing Large-Scale Social Networks* (pp. 241–266). IGI Global. doi:10.4018/978-1-5225-2814-2.ch015

Cordón-García, J. A., Gómez-Díaz, R., García-Rodríguez, A., & Dantas, T. (2018). Operation Patterns in Recommendation Systems. *Journal of Information Technology Research, 11*(4), 16–31. doi:10.4018/JITR.2018100102

Cui, T. Wang, X. & Teo, H. (2017). Is the Web Site Well Structured? In (Ed.), Handbook of Research on Technology Adoption, Social Policy, and Global Integration (pp. 178-204). IGI Global. http://doi:10.4018/978-1-5225-2668-1.ch010

Dash, A. R., & Patra, M. R. (2018). Ensuring Quality of Web Portals Through Accessibility Analysis. In I. Bouchrika, N. Harrati, & P. Vu (Eds.), *Learner Experience and Usability in Online Education* (pp. 194–234). IGI Global. doi:10.4018/978-1-5225-4206-3.ch008

Dharmalingam, J. M., & Eswaran, M. (2018). An Agent Based Intelligent Dynamic Vulnerability Analysis Framework for Critical SQLIA Attacks. *International Journal of Intelligent Information Technologies, 14*(3), 56–82. doi:10.4018/IJIIT.2018070104

Dhavale, S. (2019). *Web Server Hacking*. IGI Global. doi:10.4018/978-1-5225-7628-0.ch008

Dillon, S., Rastrick, K., Stahl, F., & Vossen, G. (2018). Using the Web While Offline. In A. Elçi (Ed.), *Handbook of Research on Contemporary Perspectives on Web-Based Systems* (pp. 108–124). IGI Global. doi:10.4018/978-1-5225-5384-7.ch006

Ferdous, M. S., Chowdhury, S., & Jose, J. M. (2017). Geo-Tagging News Stories Using Contextual Modelling. *International Journal of Information Retrieval Research, 7*(4), 50–71. doi:10.4018/IJIRR.2017100104

Gao, R., & Ye, L. (2018). Design and Development of Member Platform of Public Platform for Service Outsourcing Association. *International Journal of Advanced Pervasive and Ubiquitous Computing, 10*(1), 1–22. doi:10.4018/ IJAPUC.2018010101

Garcia-Robledo, A., Diaz-Perez, A., & Morales-Luna, G. (2018). *The Need for HPC Computing in Network Science*. IGI Global. doi:10.4018/978-1-5225-3799-1.ch001

Garcia-Robledo, A., Diaz-Perez, A., & Morales-Luna, G. (2018). *Trends and Challenges in Large-Scale HPC Network Analysis*. IGI Global. doi:10.4018/978-1-5225-3799-1.ch006

Gaur, V., Dhyani, P., & Rishi, O. P. (2017). Client-Centric Cloud Service Composition. In O. P. Rishi & A. Sharma (Eds.), *Maximizing Business Performance and Efficiency Through Intelligent Systems* (pp. 144–166). IGI Global. doi:10.4018/978-1-5225-2234-8.ch008

Ge, J., He, W., Chen, Z., Liu, C., Peng, J., & Chen, G. (2018). A Fine-Grained Stateful Data Analytics Method Based on Resilient State Table. *International Journal of Software Science and Computational Intelligence, 10*(2), 66–79. doi:10.4018/IJSSCI.2018040105

Giovanelli, S. E. (2019). Online Representation of Culinary Heritage in Turkey in the Context of Cultural Policies. In B. Önay Dogan & D. Gül Ünlü (Eds.), *Handbook of Research on Examining Cultural Policies Through Digital Communication* (pp. 31–54). IGI Global. doi:10.4018/978-1-5225-6998-5.ch002

Goyal, M., & Krishnamurthi, R. (2019). An Enhanced Integration of Voice-, Face-, and Signature-Based Authentication System for Learning Content Management System. In A. Kumar (Ed.), *Biometric Authentication in Online Learning Environments* (pp. 70–96). IGI Global. doi:10.4018/978-1-5225-7724-9.ch004

Guimaraes, T., Caccia-Bava, M. D., & Guimaraes, V. (2020). Human Factors Affecting HMS Impact on Nurses Jobs. *International Journal of Healthcare Information Systems and Informatics, 15*(1), 63–80. doi:10.4018/ IJHISI.2020010104

Gupta, A. & Verma, R. (2017). Securities Perspective in ESB-Like XML-Based Attacks. In Exploring Enterprise Service Bus in the Service-Oriented Architecture Paradigm (pp. 97-115). IGI Global. http://doi:10.4018/978-1-5225-2157-0.ch007

Gupta, S., & Gupta, B. B. (2017). Detection, Avoidance, and Attack Pattern Mechanisms in Modern Web Application Vulnerabilities. *International Journal of Cloud Applications and Computing, 7*(3), 1–43. doi:10.4018/IJCAC.2017070101

Imarhiagbe, B. O., Saridakis, G., & Smallbone, D. (2019). Firm Growth. In O. L. Rua (Ed.), *Entrepreneurial Orientation and Opportunities for Global Economic Growth* (pp. 187–221). IGI Global. doi:10.4018/978-1-5225-6942-8.ch009

Islam, M. N., Ahmed, M. A., & Islam, A. N. (2020). Chakuri-Bazaar: A Mobile Application for Illiterate and Semi-Literate People for Searching Employment. *International Journal of Mobile Human Computer Interaction, 12*(2), 22–39. doi:10.4018/IJMHCI.2020040102

Iurato, G. (2018). *First Attempts to Formalize Some Main Aspects of Psychoanalysis.* IGI Global. doi:10.4018/978-1-5225-4128-8.ch004

Jindal, H., & Sardana, N. (2017). An Empirical Analysis of Web Navigation Prediction Techniques. *Journal of Cases on Information Technology, 19*(1), 1–14. doi:10.4018/jcit.2017010101

Kamal, S., Nasir, J. A., Uddin, Z., & Khan, B. (2019). Evidential Learning on Web Search Queries Disambiguation for Active Strategic Decision Making. In Y. H. Mughal & S. Kamal (Eds.), *Servant Leadership Styles and Strategic Decision Making* (pp. 186–196). IGI Global. doi:10.4018/978-1-5225-4996-3.ch008

Kashyap, R. (2020). Medical Imaging Importance in the Real World. In R. Kashyap & A. Kumar (Eds.), *Challenges and Applications for Implementing Machine Learning in Computer Vision* (pp. 136–162). IGI Global. doi:10.4018/978-1-7998-0182-5.ch006

Katt, B., & Prasher, N. (2019). Quantitative Security Assurance. In M. Felderer & R. Scandariato (Eds.), *Exploring Security in Software Architecture and Design* (pp. 15–46). IGI Global. doi:10.4018/978-1-5225-6313-6.ch002

Khan, N. S., Muaz, M. H., Kabir, A., & Islam, M. N. (2019). A Machine Learning-Based Intelligent System for Predicting Diabetes. *International Journal of Big Data and Analytics in Healthcare*, *4*(2), 1–20. doi:10.4018/IJBDAH.2019070101

Khan, S. (2019). Virtual Reality in Visual Analytics of Large Datasets. In M. D. Lytras, N. Aljohani, L. Daniela, & A. Visvizi (Eds.), *Cognitive Computing in Technology-Enhanced Learning* (pp. 252–266). IGI Global. doi:10.4018/978-1-5225-9031-6.ch012

Khapre, S. P., Chauhan, V., Tomar, V., Mahapatra, R. P., & Bansal, N. (2017). A Method of Identifying User Identity Based on Username Features. *International Journal of Handheld Computing Research*, *8*(4), 1–22. doi:10.4018/IJHCR.2017100101

Kiskis, A. (2019). Why SQL Injection Attacks Are Still Plaguing Databases. *International Journal of Hyperconnectivity and the Internet of Things*, *3*(2), 11–18. doi:10.4018/IJHIoT.2019070102

Kumar, R., Pandey, P., & Pattnaik, P. K. (2017). Discover Patterns from Web-Based Dataset. In G. Sreedhar (Ed.), *Web Data Mining and the Development of Knowledge-Based Decision Support Systems* (pp. 78–106). IGI Global. doi:10.4018/978-1-5225-1877-8.ch006

Lai, P. (2019). Factors That Influence the tourists' or Potential Tourists' Intention to Visit and the Contribution to the Corporate Social Responsibility Strategy for Eco-Tourism. *International Journal of Tourism and Hospitality Management in the Digital Age*, *3*(2), 1–21. doi:10.4018/IJTHMDA.2019070101

Lu, C. (2017). Design and Implementation of the Instant Messaging Tool Based on JAVA. *International Journal of Advanced Pervasive and Ubiquitous Computing*, *9*(2), 16–44. doi:10.4018/IJAPUC.2017040102

Makemson, J. (2017). Technology and Created Spaces. In L. N. Hersey & B. Bobick (Eds.), *Handbook of Research on the Facilitation of Civic Engagement through Community Art* (pp. 192–217). IGI Global. doi:10.4018/978-1-5225-1727-6.ch010

Malhotra, S., Doja, M. N., Alam, B., & Alam, M. (2018). Skipnet-Octree Based Indexing Technique for Cloud Database Management System. *International Journal of Information Technology and Web Engineering*, *13*(3), 1–13. doi:10.4018/IJITWE.2018070101

Manikandakumar, M. (2020). Smart Cataract Detector. In M. Gul, E. Celik, S. Mete, & F. Serin (Eds.), *Computational Intelligence and Soft Computing Applications in Healthcare Management Science* (pp. 246–262). IGI Global. doi:10.4018/978-1-7998-2581-4.ch011

Maniyar, C. B., Bhatt, C. M., Pandit, T. N., & Yadav, D. H. (2019). CHEERBOT. In I. Comşa & R. Trestian (Eds.), *Next-Generation Wireless Networks Meet Advanced Machine Learning Applications* (pp. 306–322). IGI Global. doi:10.4018/978-1-5225-7458-3.ch013

Mehrotra, D., Nagpal, R., & Bhatia, P. K. (2017). Identification of Criteria Affecting the Usability of Academic Institutes Websites. *International Journal of Technology Diffusion*, *8*(3), 20–40. doi:10.4018/IJTD.2017070102

Menaceur, S., Derdour, M., & Bouramoul, A. (2020). Using Query Expansion Techniques and Content-Based Filtering for Personalizing Analysis in Big Data. *International Journal of Information Technology and Web Engineering*, *15*(2), 77–101. doi:10.4018/IJITWE.2020040104

Merabet, M., Benslimane, S. M., Barhamgi, M., & Bonnet, C. (2018). A Predictive Map Task Scheduler for Optimizing Data Locality in MapReduce Clusters. *International Journal of Grid and High Performance Computing*, *10*(4), 1–14. doi:10.4018/IJGHPC.2018100101

Modi, K. J., Garg, S., & Chaudhary, S. (2019). An Integrated Framework for RESTful Web Services Using Linked Open Data. *International Journal of Grid and High Performance Computing*, *11*(2), 24–49. doi:10.4018/IJGHPC.2019040102

Moses, J. S., & Babu, L. D. (2018). Evaluating Prediction Accuracy, Developmental Challenges, and Issues of Recommender Systems. *International Journal of Web Portals*, *10*(2), 61–79. doi:10.4018/IJWP.2018070105

Mulay, P., & Ahire, P. (2017). Knowledge Management Academic Research. In D. S. Deshpande, N. Bhosale, & R. J. Londhe (Eds.), *Enhancing Academic Research With Knowledge Management Principles* (pp. 45–91). IGI Global. doi:10.4018/978-1-5225-2489-2.ch004

Mushiri, T., & Mbowhwa, C. (2018). *Expert Systems and Fuzzy Logic*. IGI Global. doi:10.4018/978-1-5225-3244-6.ch003

Ogundoyin, O. S. (2020). Potentials of Indigenous Media Campaign Against HIV/AIDS. In K. O. Oyesomi & A. Salawu (Eds.), *Emerging Trends in Indigenous Language Media, Communication, Gender, and Health* (pp. 146–164). IGI Global. doi:10.4018/978-1-7998-2091-8.ch008

Osman, T., Mahjabeen, M., Psyche, S. S., Urmi, A. I., Ferdous, J. S., & Rahman, R. M. (2017). Application of Fuzzy Logic for Adaptive Food Recommendation. *International Journal of Fuzzy System Applications, 6*(2), 110–133. doi:10.4018/IJFSA.2017040106

Pandey, V., & Saini, P. (2019). Survey on Various MapReduce Scheduling Algorithms. In B. Gupta & D. P. Agrawal (Eds.), *Handbook of Research on Cloud Computing and Big Data Applications in IoT* (pp. 499–515). IGI Global. doi:10.4018/978-1-5225-8407-0.ch022

Pillai, S. P., Prasanth, V. S., & Siju, V. (2020). Extent of Information Literacy in the Higher Education Scenario. In J. J. Jesubright & P. Saravanan (Eds.), *Innovations in the Designing and Marketing of Information Services* (pp. 104–119). IGI Global. doi:10.4018/978-1-7998-1482-5.ch008

Potey, M. A., & Sinha, P. K. (2017). Personalization Approaches for Ranking. *International Journal of Information Retrieval Research, 7*(1), 1–16. doi:10.4018/IJIRR.2017010101

Raina, V. (2017). *Mobile Handset Technology*. IGI Global. doi:10.4018/978-1-5225-2306-2.ch004

Ramadhas, G., & Suman Sankar, A. S. (2020). Attitude of Library and Information Science Professionals Towards Resource Sharing and Networking of Academic Libraries. In J. J. Jesubright & P. Saravanan (Eds.), *Innovations in the Designing and Marketing of Information Services* (pp. 74–90). IGI Global. doi:10.4018/978-1-7998-1482-5.ch006

Revathi, T., Muneeswaran, K., & Blessa Binolin Pepsi, M. (2019). *Hadoop Tools*. IGI Global. doi:10.4018/978-1-5225-3790-8.ch009

Roy, M. B. (2017). A College Reaching Out to Society. In B. P. Narasimharao, E. Wright, S. Prasad, & M. Joshi (Eds.), *Handbook of Research on Science Education and University Outreach as a Tool for Regional Development* (pp. 289–312). IGI Global. doi:10.4018/978-1-5225-1880-8.ch020

Sahoo, S., Sahoo, B., Turuk, A. K., & Mishra, S. K. (2017). Real Time Task Execution in Cloud Using MapReduce Framework. In A. K. Turuk, B. Sahoo, & S. K. Addya (Eds.), *Resource Management and Efficiency in Cloud Computing Environments* (pp. 190–209). IGI Global. doi:10.4018/978-1-5225-1721-4.ch008

Saini, B. S., Kaur, N., & Bhatia, K. S. (2019). Position Independent Mobile User Authentication Using Keystroke Dynamics. In B. Pandey & A. Khamparia (Eds.), *Hidden Link Prediction in Stochastic Social Networks* (pp. 64–78). IGI Global. doi:10.4018/978-1-5225-9096-5.ch004

Sanyanga, T. M., Chinzvende, M. S., Kavu, T. D., & Batani, J. (2019). Searching Objects in a Video Footage. *International Journal of ICT Research in Africa and the Middle East*, 8(2), 18–31. doi:10.4018/IJICTRAME.2019070102

Saravanan, P. (2018). Association Between Information Literacy and Growth of Scientific Literature. In J. J. Jeyasekar & P. Saravanan (Eds.), *Innovations in Measuring and Evaluating Scientific Information* (pp. 1–15). IGI Global. doi:10.4018/978-1-5225-3457-0.ch001

Sarhan, A., & Ramadan, A. (2020). Continuous User Authentication on Touchscreen Using Behavioral Biometrics Utilizing Machine Learning Approaches. In B. B. Gupta & D. Gupta (Eds.), *Handbook of Research on Multimedia Cyber Security* (pp. 243–281). IGI Global. doi:10.4018/978-1-7998-2701-6.ch013

Sathiyamoorthi, V. (2017). Challenges and Issues in Web-Based Information Retrieval System. In N. K. Kamila (Ed.), *Advancing Cloud Database Systems and Capacity Planning With Dynamic Applications* (pp. 176–194). IGI Global. doi:10.4018/978-1-5225-2013-9.ch008

Sayan, A., & Aksan, G. E. (2020). Fan Culture in the Digital Age. In C. L. Wang (Ed.), *Handbook of Research on the Impact of Fandom in Society and Consumerism* (pp. 357–377). IGI Global. doi:10.4018/978-1-7998-1048-3.ch017

Shah, A., & Padole, M. C. (2020). "Saksham Model" Performance Improvisation Using Node Capability Evaluation in Apache Hadoop. In A. Haldorai & A. Ramu (Eds.), *Big Data Analytics for Sustainable Computing* (pp. 206–230). IGI Global. doi:10.4018/978-1-5225-9750-6.ch012

Shahriar, H., Clincy, V., & Bond, W. (2018). Classification of Web-Service-Based Attacks and Mitigation Techniques. In Y. Maleh (Ed.), *Security and Privacy Management, Techniques, and Protocols* (pp. 360–378). IGI Global. doi:10.4018/978-1-5225-5583-4.ch015

Sidhu, M. (2020). *Advanced Augmented Reality TAPS Software for Visualizing 4BL Mechanisms with Touch to Print Technique.* IGI Global. doi:10.4018/978-1-7998-0465-9.ch008

Singh, V. (2019). Predicting Search Intent Based on In-Search Context for Exploratory Search. *International Journal of Advanced Pervasive and Ubiquitous Computing, 11*(3), 53–75. doi:10.4018/IJAPUC.2019070104

Singhal, S., Sharma, P., Aggarwal, R. K., & Passricha, V. (2018). A Global Survey on Data Deduplication. *International Journal of Grid and High Performance Computing, 10*(4), 43–66. doi:10.4018/IJGHPC.2018100103

Sözcü, İ. (2020). Constructivism. In Ş. Orakcı (Ed.), *Paradigm Shifts in 21st Century Teaching and Learning* (pp. 20–35). IGI Global. doi:10.4018/978-1-7998-3146-4.ch002

Sundaramurthy, A. H., Raviprakash, N., Devarla, D., & Rathis, A. (2020). Machine Learning and Artificial Intelligence. In M. Strydom & S. Buckley (Eds.), *AI and Big Data's Potential for Disruptive Innovation* (pp. 93–103). IGI Global. doi:10.4018/978-1-5225-9687-5.ch004

Tabet, K., Mokadem, R., Laouar, M. R., & Eom, S. (2017). Data Replication in Cloud Systems. *International Journal of Information Systems and Social Change, 8*(3), 17–33. doi:10.4018/IJISSC.2017070102

Tripathi, M., Shah, S., Bahal, P., Sharma, H., & Gupta, R. (2019). Smart MM. In M. D. Lytras, N. Aljohani, L. Daniela, & A. Visvizi (Eds.), *Cognitive Computing in Technology-Enhanced Learning* (pp. 225–251). IGI Global. doi:10.4018/978-1-5225-9031-6.ch011

Ueno, M., Fukuda, K., & Mori, N. (2019). Can Computers Understand Picture Books and Comics? In T. Ogata & T. Akimoto (Eds.), *Post-Narratology Through Computational and Cognitive Approaches* (pp. 318–350). IGI Global. doi:10.4018/978-1-5225-7979-3.ch008

Ughade, A. A. (2019). Personalized Location Recommendation System Personalized Location Recommendation System. *International Journal of Applied Evolutionary Computation*, *10*(1), 49–58. doi:10.4018/IJAEC.2019010104

Ur Rahman, R. & Tomar, D. S. (2020). Taxonomy of Login Attacks in Web Applications and Their Security Techniques Using Behavioral Biometrics. In Modern Theories and Practices for Cyber Ethics and Security Compliance (pp. 122-139). IGI Global. http://doi:10.4018/978-1-7998-3149-5.ch008

Ur Rahman, R. Verma, R. Bansal, H. & Singh Tomar, D. (2020). Classification of Spamming Attacks to Blogging Websites and Their Security Techniques. In Encyclopedia of Criminal Activities and the Deep Web (pp. 864-880). IGI Global. http://doi:10.4018/978-1-5225-9715-5.ch058

Uslu, Y. D., & Hancıoğlu, Y. (2020). Cultural Effects of Global Businesses and Multinational Businesses. In U. Hacioglu (Ed.), *Handbook of Research on Strategic Fit and Design in Business Ecosystems* (pp. 493–518). IGI Global. doi:10.4018/978-1-7998-1125-1.ch022

Valero-Lara, P. (2018). Programming and Computing Lattice Boltzmann Method. In P. Valero-Lara (Ed.), *Analysis and Applications of Lattice Boltzmann Simulations* (pp. 1–29). IGI Global. doi:10.4018/978-1-5225-4760-0.ch001

Vengadeswaran, S., & Balasundaram, S. R. (2018). An Optimal Data Placement Strategy for Improving System Performance of Massive Data Applications Using Graph Clustering. *International Journal of Ambient Computing and Intelligence*, *9*(3), 15–30. doi:10.4018/IJACI.2018070102

Vinodan, A., & Manalel, J. (2020). *Community and Ecotourism*. IGI Global. doi:10.4018/978-1-7998-1635-5.ch003

Vlontzos, G., Duquenne, M. N., Haas, R., & Pardalos, P. M. (2017). Does Economic Crisis Force to Consumption Changes Regarding Fruits and Vegetables? *International Journal of Agricultural and Environmental Information Systems*, *8*(1), 41–48. doi:10.4018/IJAEIS.2017010104

Wagh, R. B., & Patil, J. B. (2018). An Improved Web Page Recommendation Technique for Better Surfing Experience. *International Journal of Knowledge-Based Organizations*, *8*(4), 1–13. doi:10.4018/IJKBO.2018100101

Xiong, W., & Wu, Y. F. (2017). User Query Enhancement for Behavioral Targeting. In J. Lu & Q. Xu (Eds.), *Ontologies and Big Data Considerations for Effective Intelligence* (pp. 413–433). IGI Global. doi:10.4018/978-1-5225-2058-0.ch009

Yu, W., & Xu, C. (2018). Developing Smart Cities in China. *International Journal of Public Administration in the Digital Age*, *5*(3), 76–91. doi:10.4018/IJPADA.2018070106

Zhu, A., & Yan, W. Q. (2017). Exploring Defense of SQL Injection Attack in Penetration Testing. *International Journal of Digital Crime and Forensics*, *9*(4), 62–71. doi:10.4018/IJDCF.2017100106

Zhumatayev, N., Umarova, Z., Besbayev, G., & Zholshiyeva, A. (2020). Development and Calculation of a Computer Model and Modern Distributed Algorithms for Dispersed Systems Aggregation. *International Journal of Distributed Systems and Technologies*, *11*(2), 56–68. doi:10.4018/IJDST.2020040105

About the Author

Mostafa Alli graduated with a PhD degree of Computer Science and Technology from Department of Computer Science and Technology, Tsinghua University, Beijing, China in July 2018. He has received his master degree majored in computer application technology from Huazhong University of Science and Technology, Wuhan, China and his bachelor degree majored in software engineering from University of Science and Culture, Tehran, Iran. His research interests are included but not limited to Information retrieval, Web searching and Recommendation.

Index

Ensure Quality Research is Introduced to the Academic Community

Become an IGI Global Reviewer for Authored Book Projects

Premier Reference Source

Emerging GIS Applications for Emergency and Disaster Management

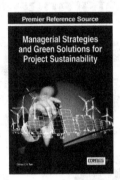

Premier Reference Source

Managerial Strategies and Green Solutions for Project Sustainability

Premier Reference Source

Comparative Approaches to Using R and Python for Statistical Data Analysis

Premier Reference Source

Solutions for High-Touch Communications in a High-Tech World

The overall success of an authored book project is dependent on quality and timely reviews.

In this competitive age of scholarly publishing, constructive and timely feedback significantly expedites the turnaround time of manuscripts from submission to acceptance, allowing the publication and discovery of forward-thinking research at a much more expeditious rate. Several IGI Global authored book projects are currently seeking highly-qualified experts in the field to fill vacancies on their respective editorial review boards:

Applications and Inquiries may be sent to:
development@igi-global.com

Applicants must have a doctorate (or an equivalent degree) as well as publishing and reviewing experience. Reviewers are asked to complete the open-ended evaluation questions with as much detail as possible in a timely, collegial, and constructive manner. All reviewers' tenures run for one-year terms on the editorial review boards and are expected to complete at least three reviews per term. Upon successful completion of this term, reviewers can be considered for an additional term.

If you have a colleague that may be interested in this opportunity, we encourage you to share this information with them.